P9-BXY-343

Engagement
of Every Child
in the Preschool
Classroom

by

R.A. McWilliam, Ph.D.

and

Amy M. Casey, Ph.D.

Center for Child and Family Research
Siskin Children's Institute
Chattanooga, Tennessee

Baltimore • London • Sydney

Paul H. Brookes Publishing Co.
Post Office Box 10624
Baltimore, Maryland 21285-0624

www.brookespublishing.com

Typeset by Integrated Publishing Solutions, Grand Rapids, Michigan.
Manufactured in the United States of America by
George H. Buchanan Printing, Bridgeport, New Jersey.

The *Improving Engagement in Preschoolers With Disabilities* project was supported by a grant from the U.S. Department of Education, Office of Special Education Programs (#H324C020095). A related project, *The Engagement Classroom: Developing a Model for Inclusion*, was also supported by a grant from the U.S. Department of Education, Office of Special Education Programs (#H324C040114). An endorsement by the U.S. Department of Education should not be assumed.

The case studies in this book are composites based on the authors' experiences. In most instances, names and identifying details have been changed to protect confidentiality. In all other cases, individuals' names and stories are used by permission.

Second printing, January 2011.

Library of Congress Cataloging-in-Publication Data

McWilliam, R.A.
Engagement of every child in the preschool classroom / by R.A. McWilliam and Amy M. Casey.
p. cm.
Includes bibliographical references and index.
ISBN-13: 978-55766-857-8
ISBN-10: 1-55766-857-4
1. Education, Preschool—United States. 2. Engagement (Philosophy) 3. Classroom management —United States. 4. Preschool teachers—in-service training—United States. I. Casey, Amy. II. Title.
LB1140.23.M39 2008
372.21—dc22 2007036523

British Library Cataloguing in Publication data are available from the British Library.

Contents

About the Authors

R.A. McWilliam, Ph.D., Director, Center for Child and Family Research, Siskin Children's Institute, 1101 Carter Street, Chattanooga, TN 37402

Dr. McWilliam is the Siskin Endowed Chair of Research in Early Childhood Education, Development, and Intervention at Siskin Children's Institute. He is also a professor of education at the University of Tennessee at Chattanooga and an adjoint professor of special education at Vanderbilt University.

Dr. McWilliam's research centers on infants, toddlers, and preschoolers with and without disabilities, with a specific focus on child engagement, service delivery models, and collaboration with families. He has shaped the definition of engagement in young children by expanding on the concept of children's being busy or not, to a sophisticated classification scheme for determining the competence level of children's observed behavior. He has also pioneered conceptual work to determine the construct validity of engagement.

Amy M. Casey, Ph.D., Research Scientist, Center for Child and Family Research, Siskin Children's Institute, 1101 Carter Street, Chattanooga, TN 37402

Dr. Casey is a research scientist at the Center for Child and Family Research, Siskin Children's Institute. She trains preschool teachers on developing classroom schedules, using incidental teaching, and rating children's engagement.

AUTHORSHIP STATEMENT

The authorship order is somewhat interchangeable. Dr. McWilliam contributed his 20 years of experience in engagement research and wrote the grant funding the study, and Dr. Casey put almost all of the words on paper and coordinated the day-to-day research on which this book is based. The weight of each author's input was equal although different.

Introduction

This manual was created to provide the early education field with a set of interventions for improving child engagement in the classroom. The interventions were first scientifically introduced as a method for improving child engagement when they were used by the *Improving Engagement in Preschoolers With Disabilities* research project, funded by the U.S. Department of Education, Office of Special Education Programs, and led by Dr. McWilliam. The interventions were expanded in the *National Individualizing Preschool Inclusion Project* (*NIPIP*) and *The Engagement Classroom* project, both of which were funded by the U.S. Department of Education and led by Dr. McWilliam. Therefore, use of the interventions has been validated by applied research (Casey & McWilliam, 2005, in press). As part of the *Improving Engagement* project, *NIPIP*, and *The Engagement Classroom* project, the interventions have been used in a variety of early childhood settings. Although the interventions in this manual have been used to improve engagement in preschoolers with disabilities, they can be used successfully with any child.

WHAT THIS MANUAL OFFERS

This manual was created because of the importance of improving child engagement and the lack of literature on the subject. Higher levels of child engagement can result in improved thinking and reasoning, improved behavior, and increased peer interaction (e.g., Berliner & Rosenshine, 1977; Favell, Favell, Reid, & Risley, 1983; Favell & Risley, 1984; Fisher & Berliner, 1985). The interventions presented here help make transitions easier for children, increase the amount of time children are engaged, and increase the sophistication of children's behavior. In addition, the methods used to determine family priorities and identify goals can affect the extent to which children's engagement can be improved. Improving classwide engagement does not benefit just children with disabilities or those who have low engagement levels; it benefits every child.

The manual offers readers the following:

- Strategies for organizing the classroom
- Strategies for scheduling staff
- Strategies for reducing misbehavior and wasted time during transitions between activities

- Strategies for helping a child work toward his or her goals, play longer, and engage in more sophisticated play
- Strategies for providing therapy in the classroom so that teachers and therapists can learn from one another
- A method for assessing a child's functioning in daily routines
- Tips for writing functional goals
- Tools for determining how a child spends his or her time during activities, how often teachers are addressing goals in the classroom, how functional goals are, and so forth
- Helpful hints and problem-solving suggestions for implementing the interventions
- Practical examples of the interventions in use

HOW TO USE THE MANUAL

The manual includes a number of items designed to improve understanding of the material. Each chapter opens with *Key Points* that alert the reader to important facts that will be presented in the chapter. Chapters conclude with *Discussion Questions,* some of which ensure that the reader understands the key components of the intervention and some of which are intended to spark discussion among classroom staff. There is also space for *Notes and Ideas* at the end of each chapter so that readers may write down personal comments. In addition, vignettes present real-world situations encountered by teachers in the classroom and practical ways to handle them.

Throughout this book, *routines* is used to refer to times of day, which in classrooms are often tantamount to activities. Therefore, routines can be arrival, snack, free play, centers, outside, nap, and so forth. *Routines* and *activities* are used interchangeably. The term *routine* has long been a feature of our work, beginning in 1992 with the publication of *Family-Centered Intervention Planning: A Routines-Based Approach* (McWilliam, 1992a). It is not restricted to activities of daily living (i.e., self-help routines such as diapering and meals).

Introduction to Engagement

What Is Engagement and Why Is It Important?

- Engagement is the amount of time children spend interacting with their environment (adults, peers, and materials) in a developmentally and contextually appropriate manner (McWilliam & Bailey, 1992). Increased engagement results in improved behavior, social interactions, and learning.
- Nonengagement refers to unoccupied behavior, such as crying, wandering without purpose, staring blankly, and aggression. Nonengagement should be avoided.
- Differentiated (or average) engagement refers to typical play with materials, participation in routines, and involvement with peers.
- Sophisticated engagement refers to complex behaviors, such as pretending; talking; problem solving; and making, creating, or building something.

DEFINITION OF ENGAGEMENT

To understand the purpose and benefits of the classroom interventions presented in this manual, an understanding of child engagement is needed. *Engagement* is defined as the amount of time children spend involved with the environment (with teachers, peers, or materials) in a way that is appropriate for the children's age, abilities, and surroundings (McWilliam & Bailey, 1992). Preschool teachers' concern with child engagement is important because it affects children's learning and the classroom environment.

The interventions in this manual were designed with a focus on child engagement because of the cognitive, social, and behavioral benefits of increased engagement levels. Research has shown that increases in children's engagement are related to positive outcomes in thinking and reasoning skills, behavior, and interactions with others (e.g., Berliner & Rosenshine, 1977; Favell, Favell, Reid, & Risley, 1983; Favell & Risley, 1984; Fisher & Berliner, 1985). Children with disabilities tend to spend less time engaged with adults, peers, and materials and more time nonengaged than children without disabilities (McWilliam & Bailey, 1995). Therefore, increasing engagement may help children meet their individualized goals in a variety of areas.

Because increases in children's engagement are related to positive changes in behavior, improving engagement also promotes a better classroom environment. When children are actively engaged with their environment, they interact with others more, manipulate materials more, and therefore learn more. Increasing levels of engagement lowers the amount of aggression and off-task behaviors displayed by children. Thus, improved engagement results in a more pleasant classroom environment that is conducive to learning and less compliance oriented.

Engagement has been organized into empirically validated levels to enable teachers and researchers to describe children's behavior accurately (McWilliam & de Kruif, 1998). The levels of engagement form a continuum of behavior complexity, from nonengagement to sophisticated engagement. The goal of improving engagement is to increase both the amount and sophistication of engagement. Sophisticated engagement includes pretending, talking about someone or something that is not present, and persistence. Conversely, nonengagement includes such behaviors as crying, acting aggressively, waiting needlessly, and wandering around the classroom without a purpose. Sophisticated engagement includes the most complex behaviors in a child's repertoire; therefore, improving engagement includes promoting sophisticated engagement. Behaviors classified as *nonengagement* include the least complex behaviors in a child's repertoire, and therefore improving engagement relies on decreasing the amount of nonengagement displayed by a child.

Levels of Engagement

Three programs have been involved in developing the concept of engagement *sophistication.* First, from 1983 to 1988, Project SUNRISE at the Family, Infant and Preschool Program at Western Carolina Center took the concept of engagement classification from a simple bivariate notion of engaged versus nonengaged (McWilliam, Trivette, & Dunst, 1985) and separated engaged behavior into active and passive engagement (Dunst, McWilliam, & Holbert, 1986). During this time, Dunst and McWilliam (1988) published "Cognitive Assessment of Multiply Handicapped Young Children," a chapter that classified behavior into five levels based on early child development theorists' classifications. The assessment method described in that chapter, called The OBSERVE, was highly influential in what was to become the final organization of engagement behavior.

Second, from 1988 to 2002, the engagement work at the FPG Child Development Institute at the University of North Carolina at Chapel Hill resulted in a nine-level classification system of engagement coding still used today, called the E-Qual III (McWilliam & de Kruif, 1998). During this period, the frequently cited chapter "Promoting Engagement and Mastery" (McWilliam & Bailey, 1992) was published.

Third, in the last few years, at the Vanderbilt Center for Child Development, we have experimented with electronic real-time coding of engagement, applying the coding system to single-subject experimental designs and then tackling the daunting task of resimplifying the measurement of engagement to make it feasible for classroom teachers to rate engagement (see Chapter 11). For more detailed information about the history and theory of engagement, see Appendix A.

As mentioned, the E-Qual III system of categorizing engagement divides children's behavior into nine levels. These levels demonstrate the continuum of sophistication that teachers and other professionals should know about when interacting with young children. The nine engagement levels consist of nonengagement, casual attention, undifferentiated behavior, focused attention, differentiated behavior, constructive behavior, encoded behavior, symbolic behavior, and persistence.

For ease in discussing engagement, multiple levels are often grouped according to the sophistication of the behaviors. Differentiated behavior is average participation appropriate for a given context. Behaviors more advanced than average forms of participation are termed *sophisticated;* constructive, encoded, symbolic, and persistent behavior fall into this category. In general, behaviors less advanced than average forms of participation are termed *unsophisticated* (i.e., casual attention and undifferentiated behavior), although focused attention and nonengagement have their own categories because of their distinctive characteristics. The placement of the engagement levels on a developmental hierarchy is shown in Figure 1.1.

Nonengagement

As stated previously, nonengagement refers to unoccupied behavior, such as 1) waiting needlessly (i.e., not in a turn-taking situation); 2) waiting even though the child knows what is coming next and is anticipating the activity (e.g., sitting at the table waiting for food); 3) staring blankly; 4) wandering without a purpose; 5) crying, whining, and so forth; 6) displaying aggressive or destructive acts; and 7) breaking sensible rules (e.g., throwing or kicking toys). In general, if the child is doing something the adult does not want him or her to be doing, the level of engagement is probably nonengagement.

Casual Attention

Casual attention is a form of unsophisticated engagement and includes relaxed and wide-ranging attention. At this level of engagement, the child must be looking at something for a total of at least 3 seconds; however, the child is attending to a sequence or a range of things in a se-

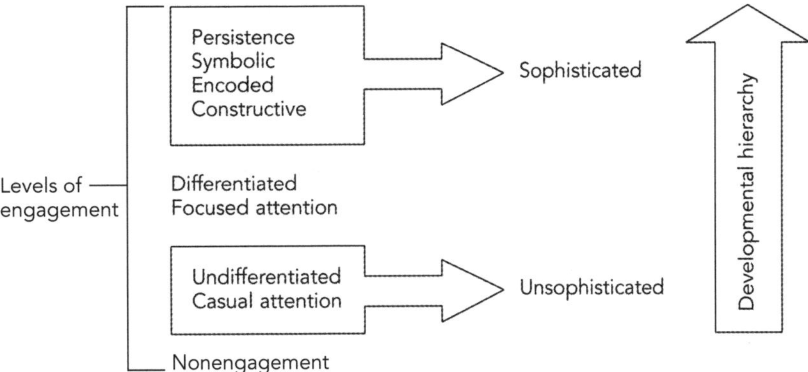

Figure 1.1. E-Qual III engagement levels.

quence within the 3 seconds as opposed to attending to one object or person. For example, a child may look around the room to see what activity centers are open or where a favorite peer is playing.

Undifferentiated Behavior

When a child displays undifferentiated behavior, he or she interacts with the environment without changing the characteristics of his or her behavior (i.e., performs a behavior in a repetitive manner), using simple, low-level behaviors. This level of unsophisticated engagement includes repetitive behaviors to elicit change in the environment or to maintain feedback produced by the child's own actions. Undifferentiated behavior is not necessarily negative; for instance, it is developmentally appropriate for young toddlers. Examples of undifferentiated behavior include rolling a car back and forth repeatedly in the same direction or shaking a rattle repeatedly.

Focused Attention

Focused attention includes watching or listening to features in the environment and must involve directly looking at a feature. Attention must be sustained for at least 3 seconds. Focused attention is characterized by a serious facial expression and a quieting of motor activity extraneous to the task at hand. The child responds to a narrow range of stimuli, which implies greater selectivity and greater intensity than more casual attention. The most common example of focused attention in a preschool classroom is listening to a story during circle time.

Differentiated Behavior

Differentiated behavior involves doing a number of different things with one's body or with language as opposed to the repeated behavior seen in undifferentiated engagement. In some studies, this level of engagement has been called "participation" because it entails behavior appropriate for the context. The participation can take as many forms as there are contexts, but according to our coding scheme it does not include the more sophisticated levels described next.

Constructive Behavior

Constructive behavior applies only to play with materials. It includes manipulating objects to create, make, or build something—putting objects together in some type of spatial form (not just handling an object). Constructive behavior is a sophisticated form of engagement and must include some indication of intentionality. Examples of constructive behavior include drawing a picture of something or building a tower with blocks.

Encoded Behavior

Encoded behavior is a sophisticated level of engagement and applies to social behaviors. It most often includes the use of understandable language (including sign language) to communicate. An important aspect of encoded behavior is that it must be context bound; in other words, the child must communicate about objects or events in the immediate environment. If a child talks about what a peer is doing at the art table, he or she is displaying encoded behavior.

Symbolic Behavior

Symbolic behavior includes the use of conventional forms of behavior (e.g., language, pretend play, sign language, drawings) to talk about the past, talk about the future, and construct new forms of expression through combinations of different symbols and signs. The major characteristic of symbolic behavior is *decontextualization,* or the capability to communicate about something or someone not physically present. In the case of pretend play, the child's behavior must involve 1) talking in character, 2) substituting objects for other objects, or 3) acting out a scenario. Symbolic behavior includes talking about a trip that was taken last week or using a block to "brush" a doll's hair.

Persistence

Persistent behavior is the most sophisticated level of engagement. It must involve problem solving and some challenge to overcome, often indicated by a failed first attempt. It involves either changing strategies or using the same strategy again to solve the problem or reach a goal.

Developmental Hierarchy

These levels of engagement, ranging from nonengagement to persistence, form a developmental hierarchy; in other words, age-related changes are associated with engagement. The most sophisticated levels of engagement would not be expected from an infant, meaning low levels of engagement are not necessarily inappropriate. Likewise, large amounts of time displaying very low levels of engagement would not be developmentally appropriate for a typically developing 5-year-old child. Figure 1.1 can be reviewed to see how the levels of engagement range from low to high and correspond with developmental changes.

WHAT EXPERIENCE HAS TAUGHT US ABOUT ENGAGEMENT

Since 2002, we have studied methods for improving the engagement of preschoolers with disabilities. The interventions we have asked teachers to carry out are described throughout this book; they consist principally of the zone defense schedule, incidental teaching, and collection of engagement data.

The highly productive research team at the University of Kansas created the zone defense schedule in the 1970s, largely to prevent down time during transitions between activities (LeLaurin & Risley, 1972). The key features of the zone defense schedule, described fully in Chapter 4, are 1) assigning adults to specific activities and locations of the room; 2) organizing the schedule with main activities (versus many different free-choice activities at one time); 3) free choice within activities and opt-out options for children; and 4) one adult assigned at all times to clean up, set up, and handle interruptions (Casey & McWilliam, 2005; O'Brien, 1997). For the most part, this strategy can be implemented as a modification of an existing schedule and by arriving at agreement among the adults working in a room. It requires teamwork and a balance of flexibility (e.g., following children's leads) and structure (e.g., organizing transitions to prevent nonengagement).

To make the zone defense schedule work in the classrooms in our studies, some attention to room arrangement seemed necessary. The most common problems we encountered were insufficient materials, especially toys; large open spaces in the middle of the room; decorations appealing more to adults than children; a lack of soft places; and unclear boundaries between zones. Most of these difficulties could be handled at little cost, but we have encouraged many teachers and their administrators to buy many more toys and low furniture to store the new toys and to make clearer boundaries for the zones.

Incidental teaching, as defined here, is principally the same as Hart and Risley's concept of expansions (1978, 1980). The key features of incidental teaching, described fully in Chapter 7, are 1) setting up the environment to promote children's interest, 2) observing children's interest, 3) following children's leads to elicit elaboration of their initial behavior, and 4) responding to their elaboration to complete the learning trial (VanDerHeyden, Snyder, Smith, Sevin, & Longwell, 2005). We discovered that some children with disabilities were receiving only a couple of occurrences of incidental teaching per hour, so, in addition to consulting with teachers about the use of this strategy, we trained them with prompts and feedback to increase the rate of use. When audible prompts (metallic clickers) proved too distracting, we switched to a feedback procedure to raise teachers' awareness. This procedure involved showing them data on their rate of incidental teaching (Casey & McWilliam, in press).

Data feedback was also the rationale behind having teachers collect engagement data. Teachers were trained to document children's engagement with adults, peers, and materials as well as the sophistication level of engagement in each activity, using the Scale for Teachers' Assessment of Routines Engagement (STARE; McWilliam, 2000). The purpose was not to use these engagement data as outcome data but to heighten teachers' awareness of engagement; we used more systematic measurement methods to collect child engagement data as outcomes. With the STARE, teachers collect data on one child a day, all day long. Although it takes only a few seconds to complete at the end of each activity, some teachers found this more feasible than did others.

SUMMARY

Engagement is the amount of time children spend interacting with their environment in a developmentally and contextually appropriate way. Engagement has been organized by levels that form a continuum of types of behavior from nonengagement to persistence. Improving engagement can have positive effects on children's behavior, thinking and reasoning skills, and peer relationships.

Discussion Questions

1. What is engagement?
2. Name and define three levels of engagement.
3. What is the average level of engagement in your classroom?
4. What level of engagement does the child in your classroom who is the lowest functioning display?
5. What level of engagement does the child in your classroom who is the highest functioning display?
6. What average level of engagement would you like to create in your classroom?
7. What changes need to be made to your classroom to give it a focus on engagement?

Notes and Ideas

Classwide Strategies for Improving Engagement

Chapter 2

Creating a Classroom Environment that Supports Engagement

Key Points

To create an environment that supports children's engagement, do the following:

- Break up the middle of the classroom.
- Avoid wide-open, empty spaces.
- Place materials at low levels, where children have access to them.
- Rotate toys and activities frequently.

GILLIAN, A FIRST-YEAR preschool teacher, spent the weekend before the start of school working in her new classroom decorating the walls, organizing the materials, and setting up the activity centers. She was extremely excited about meeting all of the children for the first time on Monday but also quite nervous. Would the children play well together? Her classroom was small, but she wanted to offer the children many activity centers to choose from. She decided to line the centers along the walls of the classroom, thinking she could maximize the space by letting all of the children play in the center of the room.

ROOM ARRANGEMENT

Altering the average engagement level in a classroom probably brings to mind a change in teaching strategies. Although teaching strategies do affect engagement levels (e.g., incidental teaching will be discussed in Chapter 7), altering the classroom environment can also affect engagement. A well-organized classroom can limit children's nonengagement during transitions between activities or during free-choice times.

The first modification in room arrangement is to break up the middle of the room. Placing a large item, furniture, or L- or T-shaped shelves in the middle of the room can do this. Breaking up the middle of the room in this way does two things. First, it prevents children from running laps in a wide-open classroom. Second, it divides the classroom into four zones, or general areas. Zones are useful for organizing centers (see next paragraph) and adult schedules (see Chapter 4 for information about zone defense scheduling).

Each zone contains several activity centers. Within a zone, it is best to array the centers throughout the area, using zone-separating furniture, instead of lining them up against the wall. In classrooms with wall-hugging activity centers, most nonengagement occurs in the wide open, shared space in the middle of the zone (although there is a need for up-to-date research on the effects of spatial density, especially for young children with disabilities in inclusive settings; Driscoll & Carter, 2004). When scattering centers throughout zones, be aware of the activity levels associated with each center. For instance, the book center (generally a quiet area) should not be located near the sand and water table (generally a more noisy, active area) because the kind of engagement found in one center is incompatible with the kind of engagement found in the other center. Zones should be marked with colors, animals, shapes, or something similar to aid in classroom management. For instance, to help children prepare for a transition from one activity to another, a teacher could give a warning that in 2 minutes everybody will go to the giraffe zone for circle time.

Avoid placing tables in the center of the room, for two reasons. First, placing tables rather than toys in the center of the room forces centers to be arranged around the edges of the room. Second, having tables and chairs in the center gives the room an academic feel and implies that children are doing table activities for a large portion of the day. The focus in inclusive preschool classrooms should be on developmentally appropriate activities, such as floor activities, play, and exploration (Bredekamp, 1987).

BY THE END OF THE FIRST week of school, Gillian had decided that something must change. The children were not playing well together, and Gillian noticed it was because they were all interested in different things and would get upset when other children accidentally invaded their space. Some of the children preferred quiet activities, and others preferred more active ones. It was not working well to have all of these activities occurring in the same part of the room. Gillian took a close look at her classroom arrangement (see Figure 2.1) and noticed that 1) quiet centers were close to noisy centers, 2) there were no boundaries between activity centers, 3) toys were too close to the circle time area, 4) shelves and containers were not labeled, 5) the tables were too far apart for children to interact during meals, and 6) the wide-open space in the middle of the room encouraged children to run around.

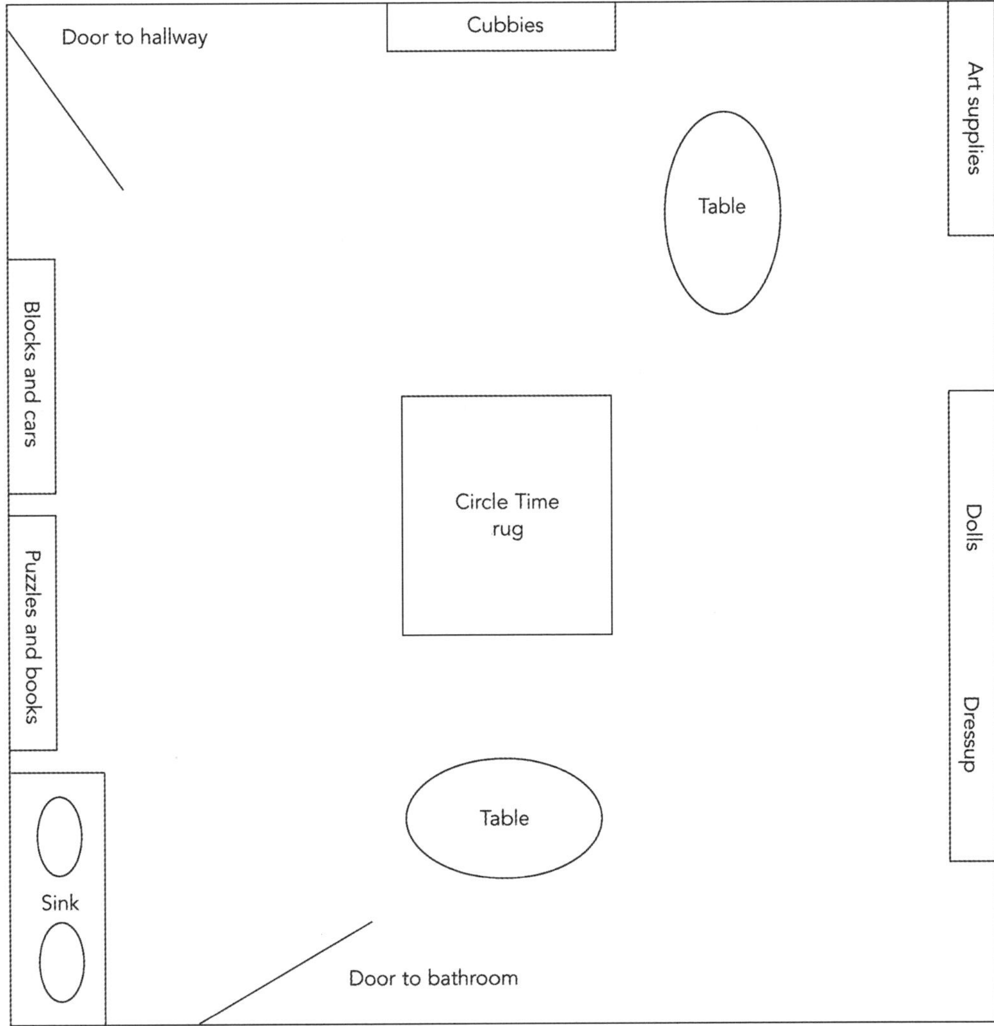

Figure 2.1. Original arrangement of Gillian's classroom.

MATERIALS

Like room arrangement, classroom materials can be used to promote children's engagement (McGee, Daly, Izeman, Mann, & Risley, 1991). Teachers should ensure that adequate materials are available for children's use. For some items often used in group activities, there should be enough that children do not need to wait for long periods of time or fight over ownership. (Of course, sometimes a teacher will deliberately set out a small amount of materials to encourage social interaction and sharing.) For free-choice times, having at least two of some toys so children can engage in parallel play is often helpful.

Materials should be placed on low shelves and be accessible to children at all times; this promotes independence. For children who cannot stand, all materials should be placed at their seated level or lower. It is also a good idea to put children's cubbies and coat hooks at low levels so the children have access not only to enjoyable activities but also to self-help activities. Preferred items might be deliberately placed on high shelves, however, to encourage children to communicate.

The children's perspective should also be used when decorating the classroom walls. Hang posters, family photographs, children's artwork, and other decorations low so children can easily see them. Doing so will prompt questions and conversations.

If enough toys are present to rotate periodically in and out of the classroom, children will constantly have new materials to explore. Although this can be a financial burden, teachers within a center can collaborate and purchase toys that are appropriate for multiple classrooms and develop a borrowing system.

AFTER THE FIRST WEEK of school, Gillian spent the weekend rearranging her classroom to prevent the behavior problems that were the direct result of environmental characteristics. The following week, she realized that her new classroom arrangement (see Figure 2.2) did a much better job of promoting engagement. The shelves, containers, and cubbies were labeled so children could find materials and clean them up independently. With the tables closer together, the children were interacting more during meals. In fact, children were interacting more during play, too. Gillian found that giving the activity centers distinct boundaries helped to keep the children who were involved in noisy activities from disturbing those who were involved in quiet activities; within centers, however, children played together more frequently

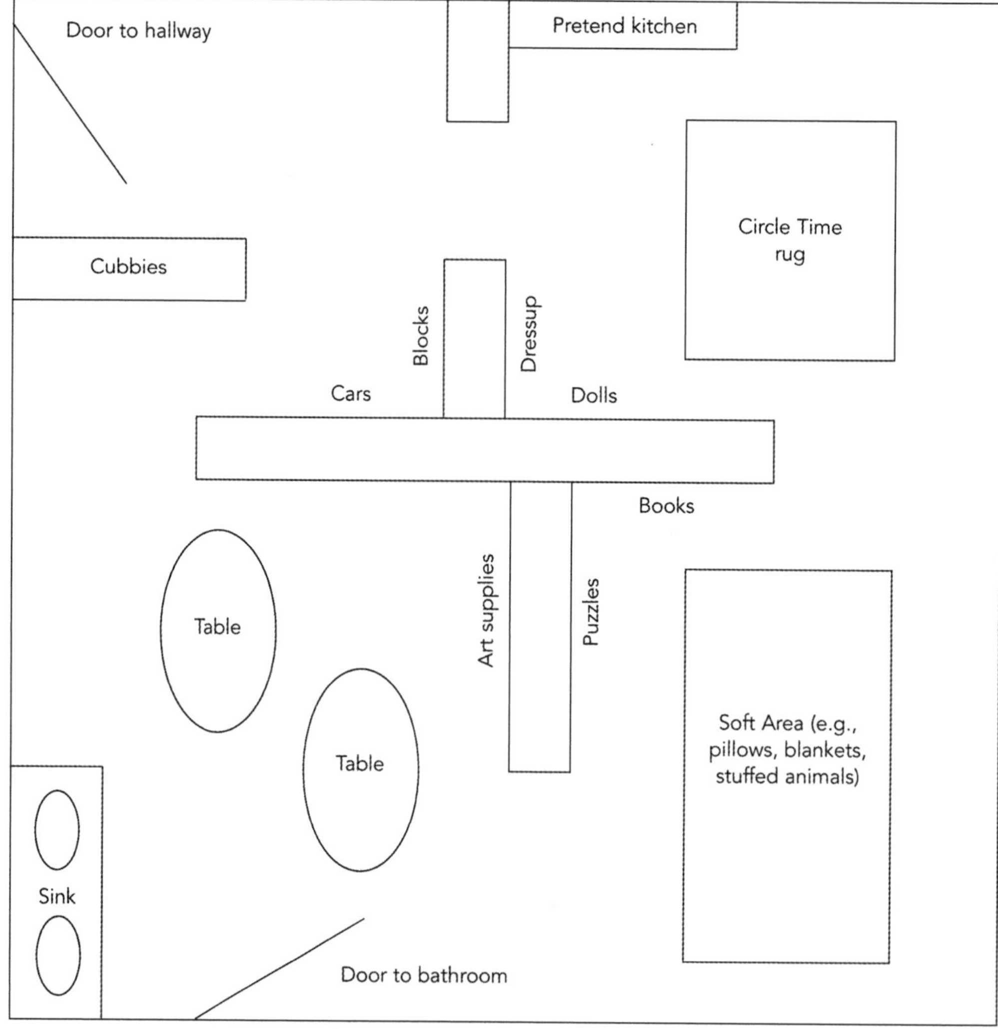

Figure 2.2. Gillian's classroom arranged with child engagement in mind.

because they were in close proximity to others who were interested in the same activity. There was less running in the room and fewer children wandering aimlessly because there were no wide-open, empty spaces between centers. In addition, a soft area Gillian had added gave children a break from the rest of the classroom.

SUMMARY

The layout of the classroom environment and availability of appropriate materials can affect children's engagement levels. When organizing the classroom, create distinct zones of activity centers; eliminate large, empty spaces; pull centers and activities away from the walls; provide ample materials; and keep decorations and toys at a low, accessible level. Appropriate arrangement of the environment to support engagement is a necessary precursor to organizing adults' roles and children's activities in a zone defense schedule, as is explained in Chapter 4.

Discussion Questions

1. Why is it important to avoid large amounts of empty space in the classroom?
2. What are the advantages to making materials accessible to children?
3. Does your current classroom environment allow children to be independent?
4. Does your current classroom environment have "problem areas" (i.e., areas in which problem behaviors occur frequently)?
   a. What might account for the behaviors being displayed?
   b. What changes can you make to eliminate problem areas?
5. Does your current classroom environment have an academic or engagement feel?
   a. Why?
   b. What changes can you make to encourage child engagement?

Notes and Ideas

Planning Activities that Encourage Engagement

- Organize the classroom day by activities; a major goal is to promote the engagement of every child during every activity. Of course, not every child will be equally engaged in every activity, but the *goal* is still valid.
- Plan activities that allow every member of the classroom to do something meaningful.
- Plan activities that involve purposeful actions, with some challenge.
- Plan activities that promote children's self-reliance.
- Plan activities that promote children's communication and positive interaction with others.
- Keep track of the percentage of children who are busy in each activity.
- Keep track of the level of sophistication of engagement displayed by individual children.

HILLARY DISLIKED PLANNING activities for her class of toddlers and preschoolers. She felt uncreative, and planning took time away from her social life, watching television, and being with her new husband. Then she went to a workshop about organizing planning around three ideas: participation of all children, themes, and established curricula. She had looked at curriculum books in the past, but no single book had seemed to fit her eclectic approach to planning activities and the diversity of abilities in her classroom. This workshop, however, gave Hillary permission not to follow any one curriculum religiously but to use a number of them to 1) find developmentally appropriate ideas (e.g., art activities suitable for 36- to 43-month-olds), 2) remind her of the typical developmental sequence of skills, and 3) give her ideas for themes. She then set her themes for the year based on what she knew interested many of her children, found suitable activity ideas, and concentrated on helping all children participate as much as possible. Hillary no longer hated planning. It was now easy and almost fun.

ENCOURAGE CHILDREN'S PARTICIPATION

Where do teachers get their ideas for activities? Countless curriculum and activity books exist, so in this book we try not to improve upon them. Instead, we offer guidelines for selecting activities from these books. Our guidelines are influenced by the concept of developmentally appropriate practice, proponents of which (Bredekamp, Knuth, Kunesh, & Shulman, 1992) have suggested the following emphases:

- Active, hands-on learning
- Conceptual learning that leads to understanding along with acquisition of basic skills
- Meaningful, relevant learning experiences
- Interactive teaching and cooperative learning
- A broad range of relevant content, integrated across traditional subject matter divisions

Proponents of developmentally appropriate practice make clear that these emphases are to replace rote memorization, drill and practice on isolated academic skills, teacher lecture, and repetitive seatwork. Three important guidelines for encouraging children's participation are access, incidental teaching, and children's interests.

Make Activities Accessible to Children of Different Abilities

Activities that require a certain level of cognitive or physical functioning will exclude some children with disabilities, and the result will be reduced engagement. Activities should therefore allow for participation by all children. For example, the plan for circle time should include simple singing games (e.g., "The Wheels on the Bus") in which all children can participate, even if it is with assistance. During an art activity, children should be able to use different tools (e.g., hands, paintbrushes, computers) that suit their abilities and interests. Providing universal access to activities increases children's opportunities to be engaged.

Use Incidental Teaching to Promote Participation

When a child is not participating in an activity or is participating at too unsophisticated a level, the teacher can use incidental teaching to get the child engaged. During the activity, the teacher can

1. Attract the child's attention
2. Get the child to do something in the activity to which he or she is now attending

3. Encourage the child to 1) stay engaged a little longer in that behavior or 2) do something a little more sophisticated than the originally elicited behavior
4. Give the child the opportunity to continue participating, once the interaction with the teacher is over

For example, at snack time, if Lucas is sitting and looking around but not touching the food or drink, the teacher can

1. Say, "Look, Lucas! You have juice in your cup," while holding the cup for Lucas to see
2. Help Lucas hold the cup with two hands
3. Get Lucas to raise the cup toward his mouth
4. After helping him drink it, leave (very little) juice in the cup to encourage him to drink again, on his own

This might sound like simple instruction with prompts for drinking at snack, and it is, but the purpose is to get Lucas participating in snack. It is not to make sure he drinks correctly from a cup; it is to make sure he is engaged during snack and therefore has the opportunity to learn.

Offer Interesting Activities

If activities are boring for children, their engagement will be low. Teachers can choose either activities in which the children have shown previous interest or novel activities. For example, Carol often keeps some artifacts from nature in her classroom—leaves, bugs, rocks, and so forth. She has a group of 4-year-old boys who are always fascinated by bugs, so she often sets these materials out during center time to ensure that the boys have a preferred item available. She also has never given the children free access to the electronic equipment in the room, so occasionally, again during center time, she plans to let them play with a boom box that includes a radio, a cassette player, and a CD player.

These three methods of promoting children's participation—making activities accessible, using incidental teaching, and offering interesting activities—can be used with a group of children or with an individual child. If Darien is perpetually nonengaged or engaged at too low a level, his teachers can make sure he has access to people and objects, use incidental teaching to increase his participation, and offer activities they know he likes. Because engagement, or participation, encompasses all kinds of behaviors and is associated with learning, encouraging it is an excellent general approach to activity planning.

HILLARY'S CLASS INCLUDED one child who had no language, had difficulty in attending except to certain objects he obsessed over, and showed occasional outbursts when asked to make a transition. The class also included a child with precocious language, great curiosity, and the ability to read some words. The rest of the children functioned between these two behavior levels, so Hillary sought activities that involved talking, playing with objects, and the potential to exchange objects. Hillary was easing some of the children into the idea of sharing. With the child who was nonverbal, she used incidental teaching during activities to help him make choices and use simple signs. This helped keep him participating (until he got tired and tried to get away from her!), so she had to time her incidental teaching just right. For the very curious, precocious child, Hillary made sure there were books and pictures about the current theme. An onlooker might have thought this was all "just play," but Hillary was confident that she was at least creating learning opportunities by concentrating on full participation.

ENCOURAGE GOAL-DIRECTED BEHAVIOR

A special level of engagement is goal-directed or mastery behavior, in which a child tries to overcome a challenge to achieve a purpose (see McWilliam & Bailey, 1992). Toddlers increasingly (with age) appear to use goals to organize their behaviors. In one study, when toddlers between the ages of 15 and 35 months were given mastery tasks varying in the implicitness of the goal (i.e., how proximal it was), younger toddlers were just as engaged as older toddlers in tasks with implicit goals (Jennings, 2004). Older toddlers, however, were more successful in completing tasks (i.e., reaching goals).

Offer Activities that Involve Challenge

Challenges can be presented as the overall activity or a specific interaction during the activity. For example, during a dance activity, a teacher might try to get the children to hop on one foot. For the 2-year-olds in her class, this would not be easy at all. During free play, a teacher could put some toys out of children's reach but keep them visible. Children would have to request the toys to gain access to them. During dress-up, the teacher could button up the vests and dresses, making them somewhat difficult for the children to put on.

Address Persistence

It is important for young children with disabilities to learn persistence because they will face many challenges in life and need to learn to do as much for themselves as possible. During sand and water play, the teacher can plan to teach children to fill containers of different sizes and identify which have more or less. As children work to fill the containers, the teacher can encourage sticking with the task until each container is full.

Encourage Task Completion

Although it is very important not to require all children to produce the exact same picture or product, it is beneficial for children to work toward task completion. During art near Thanksgiving time, for example, the end product might be a turkey that children make by drawing the outline of their hands, with outspread fingers representing the turkey's feathers and head. Whereas one child's turkey might be very sophisticated, with a variety of colors and pasted objects, another's turkey might be very simple, with the child having made the outline of the hand and adding few embellishments. It is not important for the teacher to add embellishment so the child's turkey looks like the others; instead, give the child an opportunity to complete the task by offering a simple choice, such as choosing either a brown crayon or brown paint with which to color the turkey. All children are working toward completing a task, and the teacher is meeting the children at their current skill and interest level. In many activities, therefore, children can face challenges, learn persistence, and work toward a goal.

ENCOURAGE INDEPENDENCE

Having children be able to do things by themselves is a heavily endorsed goal of raising young children in most western cultures. Some families, however, want less independence in their children than do others. Professionals should always try to find out what the family prefers in this matter rather than assume that all families want the same amount of independence in their children.

Make Activities Accessible

To promote independence, make activities and materials accessible to children. We consistently find that the teachers with whom we consult need more materials and almost always need to place their toys and other materials within children's reach. During free play, for example, children should be able to go to a shelf and take down dolls and other figures to act out a scenario.

Observe, Teach, and Back Off

Teachers need to give children opportunities to be independent. They should observe, approach, interact, and then back off (see McWilliam, de Kruif, & Zulli, 2002). When focusing on children's independence, which in turn leads to engagement, teachers should ensure that their approach and interaction are designed to elicit independence, not simply more sophisticated performance. For example, during free play, if a child takes a puzzle from the shelf and begins inserting the pieces, the teacher can watch for when the child appears to be almost ready to abandon the puzzle. At that moment, the teacher can intervene and help the child place the piece, then encourage the child to finish the task by him- or herself. The teacher does not simply work on task completion and leave the child with nothing to do.

Use the Fewest Prompts Necessary

Teaching occurs during interaction, after teachers have observed and approached children (McWilliam et al., 2002). When prompting independence, teachers should help children with no more support than is necessary. The more competent children become, the less prompting they will need. For example, during outside play, if a child has difficulty managing the slide ladder, the teacher can tell the child to put one foot up on the next rung (verbal prompt). If the child does not respond correctly to that prompt, the teacher can tap the child on the foot or behind the knee (partial physical prompt). If the child does not respond correctly, the teacher can lift the child's foot, holding on to the child carefully, and place the foot on the next rung (full physical prompt). Making materials accessible to children, backing off to allow children to do things on their own, and using the least prompts necessary are ingredients for encouraging independence.

ENCOURAGE SOCIAL BEHAVIOR

Almost all activities should be planned to promote children's communication and positive interactions with others. Although social behavior often happens naturally, sometimes teachers need to have specific plans to ensure that children interact with their peers (not just adults and materials), cooperate with each other during play, and receive praise for displaying positive social behaviors.

Build Peer Interaction Into Activities

When planning activities, teachers should consider ways to ensure that children interact with other children to do the activities. For example, at snack or lunchtime, children can pass plates of food to each other or helpers can pour drinks. At storytime, the teacher might tell two children to act out a person riding a horse, rather than have the children each pretend to ride his or her own horse. With older children, the teacher might set out too few art materials on purpose so children have to borrow, wait, and negotiate.

Encourage Associative and Cooperative Behavior

Parten (1932) long ago realized that children first engage in solitary play, then in parallel play, then in associative play, and finally—when old enough—in cooperative play. Teachers can encourage this increasingly social behavior. For example, if a child has a pattern of playing alone during dress-up activities, the teacher could encourage parallel play by prompting another child to put on similar clothes, without prompting that child to interact with the first child. Once parallel play was occurring, the teacher could encourage associative play by asking the second child to talk to the first child about what he or she was pretending to be or dressing up as. Finally, the teacher could elicit cooperative play by encouraging the children to work together as they pretend to get the ladder off the fire truck and rescue a cat, or some similar activity.

Reinforce Appropriate Social Interactions

Teachers are often so busy offering corrective feedback and eliciting desired behaviors that they miss opportunities to praise or otherwise acknowledge prosocial behaviors. By definition, praise for these behaviors has a reinforcing effect if it increases the likelihood of the reoccurrence of the behaviors. For example, during a transition to outside time, if a child helps another child put on his coat, the teacher should verbally recognize this helpful behavior. Adult attention is powerful in motivating children. It is very important to plan activities that encourage communication and positive interaction.

MONITOR ENGAGEMENT

It is a truism that what is not reported (and therefore not measured) is not deemed important in early childhood. Teachers and other professionals should therefore monitor both group and individual engagement. Group engagement in activities can be monitored by scanning the classroom at certain intervals to determine the percentage of the group that is engaged (see Chapter 10). Individual engagement in activities can be monitored by rating a child's engagement with adults, peers, and materials and rating the complexity of the engagement, as described in Chapter 11.

CONSIDER THE CLASSROOM SCHEDULE

Teachers should plan activities with the following scheduling guidelines in mind (see Chapter 4 for a more detailed discussion of classroom scheduling):

- Plan short activities and allow them to go longer rather than plan long activities and have to shorten them when they do not work out.
- Plan medium-paced activities between fast-paced and slow-paced activities.
- Approach centers as multiple activities, some supervised by adults and some not, rather than one classwide free-for-all that is difficult to manage.

AS HILLARY BECAME more comfortable with planning for engagement, she started to think more about the instructional content of her fun activities. She noticed that when she added a challenge to an activity (e.g., "sabotaging" materials so children could not independently get them to work), some children displayed a lot of persistence and interest and others quickly gave up. So she continued to use challenges, to elicit persistence in those who rose to the occasion and to encourage children who tended not to persist to keep going. She had children clean up at the end of activities to teach them to finish tasks. Hillary also started paying attention to how often she helped children more than she needed to. As she became more sophisticated in her use of graduated prompts, she found herself letting some children do more for themselves and teaching others to do more for themselves. Finally, she started treating every activity as an opportunity to teach children to communicate and get along. Whereas before she had concentrated on getting children to do the appropriate thing with materials, she now paid more attention to children's social relationships during activities. When interactions did not happen naturally (which was often the case with the child who was nonverbal), she gently prompted children to have some type of interaction with each other, even if it was minimal. She kept track of children's engagement by completing the Scale for Teachers' Assessment of Routines Engagement (STARE) on one child each day so that, throughout the year, she had one day's profile of engagement per child every 2 or 3 weeks.

USE A PLANNING MATRIX

To organize the planning of activities to promote engagement, teachers can use the Activity Planning Matrix for Encouraging Engagement (APMEE; McWilliam, 2005a). This matrix (see Figure 3.1) is used when lessons have been tentatively planned, as explained in the planning directions. The teacher places a check mark in the cell corresponding to the planning considerations for each activity. Under each activity, in the "Which child?" cells, the teacher inserts the name or initials of a child for whom that planning consideration is important. The APMEE can also be used as a post-hoc checklist, at the end of a day or week's activities, by checking what was done rather than what is planned. (A blank APMEE form can be found on pages 135–136 in Appendix B.)

SUMMARY

Planning activities involves consideration of three major domains: engagement, independence, and social relationships. Planning for engagement involves making activities accessible to children with differing abilities; using incidental teaching to encourage more time with an activity or more sophisticated behavior; offering interesting activities; and promoting goal-directed behavior by presenting challenges, encouraging persistence, and providing opportunities for task completion. Planning for independence requires teachers to make materials accessible to children; to know when to observe, when to teach, and when to back off; and to use the minimum prompts necessary to support children's learning. Finally, when teachers plan to encourage social relationships, they should ensure that children have opportunities to interact with their peers, cooperate with each other during play, and receive praise for displaying positive social behaviors.

Discussion Questions

1. What is a major purpose of all classroom activities?
2. Is child participation in activities sufficient?
3. Why is challenge important for very young children?
4. How can self-reliance during activities be taught?
5. What activities lend themselves to communicating and getting along with others?

Activity Planning Matrix for Encouraging Engagement (APMEE)

Planning directions: When lessons have been tentatively planned, use this matrix to check (√) planning considerations addressed for each activity. For example, if you have a plan for ensuring that materials are accessible during the arrival activity, check the appropriate cell. If the planning consideration is not addressed, leave the cell blank. For each activity, complete the "Which child?" cells by putting the name or initials of a particular child for whom that planning consideration is important. See the end of the form for use of the APMEE as a post-hoc checklist.

	Activity										
Planning consideration	Arrival	Circle/ Story	Art	Snack	Outside	Centers	Free play	Toileting	Dance/ Music	Dress-up	Sand and water	Transition
Materials accessible to all?	√	√	√			√	√			√	√	
Which child?	JM	DV	JM			DV	JM			DV	JM	
Incidental teaching?	√		√	√	√	√	√		√		√	
Which child?	DV		JM	LB	DV	JM	LB		DV		JM	
Interesting activity?		√				√			√			
Which child?		DV				JM			LB			
Challenge?		√				√			√		√	
Which child?		LB				DV			JM		DV	
Address persistence?						√	√	√			√	
Which child?						JM	LB	DV			JM	
Obvious goal?			√			√				√		√
Which child?			JM			LB				DV		JM

	Activity											
Planning Consideration	Arrival	Circle/ Story	Art	Snack	Outside	Centers	Free play	Toileting	Dance/ Music	Dress-up	Sand and water	Transition
Observe and back off?	√		√		√	√				√	√	
Which child?	LB		LB		JM	LB				DV	JM	
Least prompts?		√	√	√		√		√		√		√
Which child?		DV	JM	LB		DV		JM		LB		LB
Peer interaction?			√	√		√					√	√
Which child?			LB	DV		JM					LB	LB
Associative or cooperative behavior?	√	√	√			√	√		√			
Which child?	LB	DV	JM			LB	DV		JM			
Reinforce interactions?	√			√		√	√			√	√	
Which child?	JM			LB		DV	JM			LB	DV	

Post-hoc checklist: Using a blank APMEE, review the day or week's activities and check (√) those activities in which the planning consideration was accomplished. Leave blank the cells for those activities in which the planning consideration was not accomplished. For each activity in the "Which child?" cells, write the name or initials of one child with whom the planning consideration was implemented in that activity.

Figure 3.1. Sample Activity Planning Matrix for Encouraging Engagement. (From McWilliam, R.A. [2005]. *Activity Planning Matrix for Encouraging Engagement* [APMEE]. Center for Child Development, Vanderbilt University Medical Center, Nashville, TN.)

Notes and Ideas

Chapter 4

The Zone Defense Schedule

Key Points

- Zone defense scheduling is used to organize the roles of classroom staff during routines and during transitions between activities.
- During each routine, one adult is assigned to the set-up role and is responsible for the extra classroom tasks (e.g., changing diapers, answering phone calls, handling outbursts). The other adults in the room focus on the scheduled activity and child engagement.
- During transitions, one adult is at the new activity, ready to help children get involved in the new task; another adult remains at the old activity, keeping children involved in the task until they are ready to make the transition to the next activity.
- A zone defense schedule eliminates needless waiting during transitions, therefore limiting nonengagement.
- A zone defense schedule increases the effectiveness of all classroom staff members by assigning specific duties to each person during routines and transitions between activities.
- A zone defense schedule helps to empower classroom staff by alternating weekly roles between adults, ensuring that each staff member is responsible for the same activities at some point.

DEBBIE AND CHRISTY WERE teachers in a preschool classroom of 3-year-olds. Their classroom schedule indicated that teacher-directed activities such as circle time, art project, music time, and reading were incorporated into the children's day. However, Debbie and Christy felt that they rarely completed teacher-directed activities successfully because minor situations, such as the need to give a child a diaper change or answer the phone, seemed to constantly arise and occupy both teachers' attention. Debbie and Christy noticed that the children often ended up sitting unoccupied or engaging in off-task behavior because they did not have anything to do while waiting for a teacher to return and resume the activity.

WHAT IS ZONE DEFENSE SCHEDULING?

The zone defense schedule (ZDS) is a system for organizing the staff and environment of a preschool classroom. It is used to organize the roles of adults in the classroom during both classroom activities and transitions between activities. During classroom activities, each staff member is assigned a specific role. At least one adult works directly with the children, leading the scheduled activity, while another adult completes the extra classroom tasks (e.g., cleaning, preparing activities, handling phone calls, completing diaper changes). Instructions for creating a ZDS are given later in the chapter, but a sample schedule appears in Figure 4.1 to illustrate how one adult is assigned to each scheduled activity and another adult is assigned to complete the extra classroom tasks (this person is assigned the set-up role on the schedule). During transitions between activities, staff members are also assigned to specific roles. One adult (the person who was in the set-up role) waits at the new activity center, ready to involve children in the new task, whereas another adult (the person who was leading the last activity) stays at the old activity center, keeping children occupied until they leave the task.

The term *zone defense* comes from basketball and indicates that players are responsible for an area of the court. It is contrasted with man-to-man defense, in which players are responsible for specific opponents. In preschool classrooms, man-to-man defense is equivalent to assigning certain children to a teacher. In contrast, zone defense assigns teachers to specific areas of the room. The ZDS allows children to move between teachers instead of having teachers follow children around the room.

BENEFITS OF ZONE DEFENSE SCHEDULING

Using a ZDS helps to limit the amount of time children spend nonengaged. As stated in Chapter 1, *nonengagement* refers to unoccupied behavior, such as waiting needlessly, staring blankly, wandering with no purpose, crying, whining, acting aggressively, and committing destructive acts. The ZDS helps to limit nonengagement during activities and transitions between activities.

Limited Nonengagement During Routines

Refer again to Figure 4.1. During each scheduled activity, one adult is assigned to lead the activity and one adult is assigned to the set-up role. Because the adult leading the activity is not distracted by the need to complete extra classroom tasks (this is, after all, the responsibility of the person in the set-up role), he or she is able to focus on child engagement. In other words, the adult in charge of the scheduled activity is able to devote full attention to the children and the current activity.

Allowing the adult in charge of the activity to focus on child engagement reduces the chances of nonengagement for two reasons. First, children do not have to wait for a teacher to

---

This chapter is adapted from Casey, A.M., & McWilliam, R.A. (2005). Where is everybody? Organizing adults to promote child engagement. *Young Exceptional Children, 8*(2), 2–10.

Time	Person A	Person B
8:00–8:15	*arrival*	*setup*
8:15–8:30	*setup*	*story*
8:30–8:45	*free play*	*setup*
8:45–9:00	*setup*	*circle*
9:00–9:15	*table toys*	*setup*
9:15–9:30	*setup*	*centers*
9:30–9:45	*setup*	*centers*
9:45–10:00	*snack*	*setup*
10:00–10:15	*setup*	*outside*
10:15–10:30	*setup*	*outside*
10:30–10:45	*setup*	*outside*
10:45–11:00	*music*	*setup*
11:00–11:15	*setup*	*art*
11:15–11:30	*free play*	*setup*
11:30–11:45	*setup*	*lunch*
11:45–12:00	*setup*	*lunch*
12:00–12:15	*nap*	*setup*
12:15–12:30	*nap*	*setup*
12:30–12:45	*teacher break*	*nap*
12:45–1:00	*teacher break*	*nap*
1:00–1:15	*nap*	*teacher break*
1:15–1:30	*nap*	*teacher break*
1:30–1:45	*nap*	*setup*
1:45–2:00	*nap*	*setup*
2:00–2:15	*nap*	*setup*
2:15–2:30	*setup*	*snack*
2:30–2:45	*centers*	*setup*
2:45–3:00	*centers*	*setup*
3:00–3:15	*setup*	*story*
3:15–3:30	*table toys*	*setup*
3:30–3:45	*setup*	*free play*
3:45–4:00	*setup*	*free play*
4:00–4:15	*outside*	*setup*
4:15–4:30	*outside*	*setup*
4:30–4:45	*outside*	*setup*
4:45–5:00	*outside*	*setup*

Figure 4.1. Sample two-person zone defense schedule.

return to the activity following a disruption. If a visitor arrives during circle time, for instance, one teacher will continue to conduct the group activity while the teacher in the set-up role talks with the visitor. Children are not asked to sit and wait while the teacher who was leading circle time talks with the visitor; instead, the activity continues uninterrupted. The second reason why having one adult focus on child engagement results in reduced nonengagement is that the teacher has more time to encourage sophisticated play. If a child has trouble maintaining engagement in an activity, having a teacher focused solely on the activity increases the likelihood that the teacher will be able to encourage more sophisticated play by the child. If a teacher was trying to both lead the activity and clean up from snack, for example, the amount of time he or she would have to guide a nonengaged child into more productive play would be reduced due to the demands of switching attention between the two tasks.

Limited Nonengagement During Transitions Between Activities

As mentioned previously, adults have assignments during transitions between activities when using the ZDS. The adult who was in the set-up role during the last activity and will lead the new activity is stationed in the activity zone that children are moving to. This adult is responsible for helping children get engaged as soon as they enter the new activity zone. Meanwhile, the adult who led the last activity has stayed in the old activity zone, keeping children engaged until they decide to move to the new activity. When the last child leaves the old activity zone, this adult begins the tasks associated with the set-up role, such as cleaning up the old activity.

Having adults present at both the new and old activity zones during transitions helps to ensure that children stay engaged and do not have to wait needlessly between activities. Needless waiting (in other words, nonengagement) is avoided because children do not have to wait for 1) peers to transition between activities or 2) teachers to prepare the new activity. Children are able to make transitions at their own pace because an adult is present at both the new and old activity, and they can immediately participate in the new activity. They are not required to wait for their peers to finish the previous activity so that they can transition as a group to the next activity. In addition, children are not required to wait for a teacher to clean up or put away the previous activity and then prepare the next activity before it can begin. The teacher at the new activity has the task prepared before children start transitioning, and the teacher at the old task cleans it up after the last child has left the zone. Eliminating needless waiting provides fewer opportunities for children to act aggressively, stare blankly, or engage in off-task behavior.

The goal of the ZDS is to reduce nonengaged time by eliminating transitions that require children to stand around and wait, not occupied in an activity. Research in preschool classrooms has shown that children spend 20% to 35% of their class time in transition between activities (Sainato & Lyon, 1983, as cited in Sainato, Strain, Lefebvre, & Rapp, 1987). For children who are in a classroom for 8 hours, this is equivalent to approximately 2 hours spent in transition from one activity to another; in other words, a large amount of time in which children have the potential to be nonengaged.

Research has shown that with the ZDS, children experience short transitions with high levels of participation; in contrast, with man-to-man defense, children experience long transitions with low levels of participation (LeLaurin & Risley, 1972). Researchers calculated the average amount of time lost per child (time when the child was not participating due to transitioning between activities) across four classroom activities and found that with the ZDS, the average was 9.91 minutes lost per child. Man-to-man defense, on the other hand, resulted in an average of 20.74 minutes lost per child—a number more than double that found for the ZDS. Therefore, research supports the use of the ZDS to reduce nonengaged time during transitions between activities.

Empowerment of Staff Members

In addition to limiting nonengagement, the ZDS also benefits preschool classrooms by empowering classroom staff members. The ZDS offers variety in the duties of classroom staff because roles are alternated during the day and each week. Therefore, one staff member is not always responsible for the undesirable tasks. Feelings of empowerment are promoted because all adults in the room are responsible for the same tasks at some point. The ZDS also increases the effectiveness of all classroom staff members. Each person is assigned a specific duty to complete during each activity and each transition between activities. Finally, the ZDS empowers visitors who are not usually in the classroom, such as substitute teachers, parent volunteers, high school or college students, or community members. The adults who are regularly in the classroom can quickly and easily point out the posted ZDS and ask the visitor to assume the role of Person B, for instance. The visitor knows whether he or she should be playing with children or helping with classroom tasks, instead of standing to the side and trying not to get in the way.

DESIGNING AND USING A ZONE DEFENSE SCHEDULE

A ZDS can be constructed using the existing classroom activities. The first step is to divide the day into 15- or 20-minute blocks of time. Scheduling activities for longer amounts of time is not recommended because children will become nonengaged if they lose interest in an activity. The schedule should indicate child activities in addition to teacher break times.

The second step in designing a ZDS is to review the schedule before staff assignments are made. When dividing the schedule into small blocks of time, be aware of potentially troublesome transitions. For example, scheduling a quiet activity immediately following an active activity is not advised because children do not have the chance to decrease their activity level gradually and ease into the quiet activity. Previous research in preschool classrooms has revealed that children's attention to a story is better when the activity is preceded by a low-energy activity (Krantz & Risley, 1977). In addition, children need less time for the transition and display less disruptive behavior during the transition when the story is preceded by a less energetic activity (Krantz & Risley, 1977). To avoid troublesome transitions, adjust the schedule so that an active activity follows a quiet activity or an intermediate activity falls between the active and quiet activities.

The third step in constructing a ZDS is to assign roles to classroom staff. We suggest using a template (see page 137 in Appendix B) in which activity times are listed in a column and additional columns are assigned to Person A, Person B, and possibly Person C (depending on the size of the staff). For a classroom with two adult staff, assign Person A to the set-up role for the first block of time. Assign Person B to the set-up role for the second block of time, assign Person A to the set-up role for the third block of time, and continue alternating the role between adults for the entire day. For a classroom with three adult staff, the same method of role assignment should be used, except that the set-up role should be alternated between all three adults in the room. Once the set-up role is staggered across the day, assign the remaining adult(s) to be in charge of the activity that is scheduled for each block of time. Each adult should set up for the activity that he or she will be in charge of during the next block of time. An example of a two-person schedule is shown in Figure 4.1; an example of a three-person schedule is shown in Figure 4.2.

An entire block of time should not be set aside for diaper changes or turns in the bathroom. Instead, diaper changes and use of the bathroom should occur as needed throughout the day rather than as a group activity. This prevents play from being interrupted by a routine that consists of a large percentage of time spent waiting and wandering (Leavitt & Eheart, 1985). The adult in the set-up role is responsible for taking care of the extra classroom tasks, such as diaper changes and providing assistance in the bathroom. Other duties that the set-up person com-

Time	Person A	Person B	Person C
8:00–8:15	arrival	setup	arrival
8:15–8:30	story	story	setup
8:30–8:45	setup	free play	free play
8:45–9:00	circle	setup	circle
9:00–9:15	table toys	table toys	setup
9:15–9:30	setup	centers	centers
9:30–9:45	setup	centers	centers
9:45–10:00	snack	setup	snack
10:00–10:15	outside	outside	setup
10:15–10:30	outside	outside	setup
10:30–10:45	outside	outside	setup
10:45–11:00	setup	music	music
11:00–11:15	art	setup	art
11:15–11:30	free play	free play	setup
11:30–11:45	setup	lunch	lunch
11:45–12:00	setup	lunch	lunch
12:00–12:15	nap	setup	nap
12:15–12:30	nap	setup	nap
12:30–12:45	teacher break	nap	setup
12:45–1:00	teacher break	nap	setup
1:00–1:15	setup	teacher break	nap
1:15–1:30	setup	teacher break	nap
1:30–1:45	nap	setup	teacher break
1:45–2:00	nap	setup	teacher break
2:00–2:15	nap	nap	setup
2:15–2:30	setup	snack	snack
2:30–2:45	centers	setup	centers
2:45–3:00	centers	setup	centers
3:00–3:15	story	story	setup
3:15–3:30	setup	table toys	table toys
3:30–3:45	free play	setup	free play
3:45–4:00	free play	setup	free play
4:00–4:15	outside	outside	setup
4:15–4:30	outside	outside	setup
4:30–4:45	outside	outside	setup
4:45–5:00	outside	outside	setup

Figure 4.2. Sample three-person zone defense schedule.

pletes are cleaning up the previous activity, setting up the next activity, answering the phone, greeting visitors to the classroom, handling a child having an outburst, and managing other unplanned situations. As stated previously, the adult in charge of the activity is meant to stay with the children, interacting with them and assisting them in their task or play. If the set-up person completes all extra classroom tasks, he or she joins the teacher who is leading the activity and interacts with the children.

The fourth step in designing and using a ZDS is to switch the daily roles of adults weekly (i.e., the designation of Person A, B, and C should be rotated each week) so that all adults in the room are responsible for the same tasks at some point. This gives all staff variety in the roles they perform during the day (the set-up role is alternated for each activity) and each week. Table 4.1 gives a summary of how to design a ZDS.

DEBBIE AND CHRISTY developed a ZDS that assigned each of them to specific roles during each routine of the day. While one was assigned to focus on the scheduled activity, the other (the one in the set-up role) was assigned to take care of all other classroom duties and minor situations. Part of their schedule is shown in Figure 4.3.

At 8:15, while Person A was reading a story to the class, Person B was straightening up the room after arrival and making sure toys were accessible for free play. Once she completed these tasks, she joined the reading group. If a child arrived late to class, Person B (the teacher in the set-up role) greeted the child and helped him or her join the ongoing activity.

As story time was ending, Person B went to the area of the room (i.e., the zone) designated for free play so she would be ready to engage the first child who made the transition to free play. Meanwhile, the teacher who had led storytime stayed behind and continued to engage children who had not yet transitioned to free play. Once the last child had left storytime, Person A put away the books, prepared for circle time, and then became available to interact with the children in free play.

WHAT DO I DO IF . . . ?

Can we schedule a long time for the same activity, such as 30 minutes of rotating through centers?

Yes! There are two solutions for scheduling a long time for the same activity. The first option is to have each staff member maintain a single role throughout the entire activity. Once the person in the set-up role has completed cleaning up the previous activity and preparing the next one, he or she joins the ongoing activity (of course, unplanned occurrences, such as the need for a diaper change or a visitor entering the classroom, would be handled by the person in the set-up role). The second option is to switch roles halfway through the activity. This may be a particularly

Table 4.1. Summary: How to design a zone defense schedule

Divide daily activities into 15- or 20-minute blocks of time.
Keep activity durations short.
Indicate child activities and teacher breaks.
Review the schedule, looking for potentially troublesome transitions.
Schedule active activities after quiet activities.
Insert an intermediate activity between active and quiet activities.
Assign roles to classroom staff.
Alternate the set-up role between staff members.
Each adult should set up for the activity he or she will lead next.
Weekly, alternate the roles of Persons A, B, and C.

Time	Person A	Person B
8:00–8:15	*setup*	*arrival*
8:15–8:30	*story*	*setup*
8:30–8:45	*setup*	*free play*
8:45–9:00	*circle*	*setup*

Figure 4.3. Debbie and Christy's zone defense schedule.

good option if more than one teacher-directed activity is included in the rotation through centers. If the adults switch roles halfway through, each could be in charge of a teacher-directed activity during different halves of center time instead of having one adult lead multiple activities.

?

What do we do when the person in the set-up role cannot attend to all of his or her duties at once (e.g., the next activity still has to be prepared, a child needs individual attention, and there is a phone call)?

At times, when multiple unplanned situations occur, the teacher leading the scheduled activity will need to assist the person in the set-up role. The function of the ZDS is to provide a structure for handling unplanned situations by determining who should be the first to respond. Providing this sort of structure will prevent the classroom from being unattended during unplanned situations, or at least delay the point at which all staff need to be focused on situations other than the scheduled activity. In other words, the ZDS helps to lower the frequency of situations during the day in which no adults are available to focus on child engagement.

?

How do we schedule staff when two adults work a full day and one adult works a half day?

The set-up role should be alternated among all adults in the classroom at any given time. Therefore, when two adults work a full day and one adult works a half day, the set-up role should be alternated between all three adults until one staff member leaves, at which point the set-up role should be alternated between the two remaining adults. For example, if a staff member leaves at 3:00, your schedule may look like the one shown in Figure 4.4.

In this example, all morning the set-up role is alternated between the three adults in the classroom. At 3:00, Person B leaves the classroom. Person A is in the set-up role during this transition, so he or she is responsible for cleaning up the previous activity and preparing the next one. He or she will still be present in the classroom when the activity that was prepared for occurs. Remember that adults should lead the activity they set up for. Person C had been sharing responsibility for the scheduled activity centers with Person B and takes sole responsibility for the activity when Person B departs. For the rest of the afternoon, the set-up role is alternated between Person A and Person C.

?

How do we schedule staff when we have a child in our class who needs one-on-one attention throughout the day?

First, if a classroom includes a child who needs one-to-one assistance throughout the day, it is assumed that at least three adults are assigned to the room at all times. Options for scheduling staff when one child needs one-on-one attention include 1) assigning one person to assist the child throughout the day or 2) alternating assistance for the child with the set-up role and responsibility for the scheduled activity.

The first option is to assign one person to assist the child throughout the day. The person assigned to work with the child would not participate in the alternation of the set-up role. In-

Time	Person A	Person B	Person C
2:00–2:15	setup	snack	snack
2:15–2:30	circle	setup	circle
2:30–2:45	art	art	setup
2:45–3:00	setup	centers	centers
3:00–3:15	setup		centers
3:15–3:30	outside		setup
3:30–3:45	set up		outside
3:45–4:00	outside		setup
4:00–4:15	setup		table toys
4:15–4:30	free play		setup
4:30–4:45	free play		setup

Figure 4.4. Staffing changes midday in a zone defense schedule.

stead, the other staff members would alternate being assigned to the set-up role and being assigned to the scheduled activity, freeing the third staff member to work exclusively with the child needing one-on-one assistance. The schedule would look like the one shown in Figure 4.5 (Henry is the child needing one-on-one assistance).

The second scheduling option for a classroom that includes a child who needs one-on-one attention throughout the day is to schedule staff as usual, alternating the set-up role between all staff members. Two adults would be assigned to each scheduled activity; one to take the "lead" role (responsible for focusing on engagement in the entire group of children) and one to provide assistance to the child needing one-on-one attention. The person who set up for the scheduled activity should take the lead role during the activity; therefore, the assignment of lead teacher should be alternated between adults throughout the day. The schedule (using the same activity times as the schedule in Figure 4.5) would look like the one shown in Figure 4.6.

The second option, rotating one-on-one assistance for the child among all adults in the classroom, is the preferred solution to the situation. It is better for the child because he or she learns to work with a variety of adults instead of learning to depend on one staff member for all assistance. Having the child work with a variety of adults throughout the day will help the

Time	Person A	Person B	Person C
8:00–8:15	setup	arrival	assist Henry
8:15–8:30	story	setup	Henry
8:30–8:45	setup	art	Henry
8:45–9:00	centers	setup	Henry
9:00–9:15	centers	setup	Henry
9:15–9:30	setup	table toys	Henry
9:30–9:45	circle	setup	Henry
9:45–10:00	setup	snack	Henry
10:00–10:15	outside	setup	Henry
10:15–10:30	outside	setup	Henry

Figure 4.5. Assigning an adult to assist a specific child in a zone defense schedule.

Time	Person A	Person B	Person C
8:00–8:15	setup	arrival (lead)	arrival (Henry)
8:15–8:30	story (lead)	setup	story (Henry)
8:30–8:45	art (Henry)	art (lead)	setup
8:45–9:00	setup	centers (Henry)	centers (lead)
9:00–9:15	setup	centers (Henry)	centers (lead)
9:15–9:30	table toys (lead)	setup	table toys (Henry)
9:30–9:45	circle (Henry)	circle (lead)	setup
9:45–10:00	setup	snack (Henry)	snack (lead)
10:00–10:15	outside (lead)	setup	outside (Henry)
10:15–10:30	outside (lead)	setup	outside (Henry)

Figure 4.6. Alternating adult assignments to assist a specific child in a zone defense schedule.

child generalize skills across people. The solution is also better for the staff because each adult has variety in the roles he or she fulfills. Having the opportunity to work with the child needing one-to-one attention across a variety of activities will make staff more aware of the child's needs when planning upcoming activities.

What do we do if a staff member is unable to plan activities because of inexperience?

The best solution for scheduling staff when a team member is unable to plan activities is to have other staff members model planning and train their peer. Design the ZDS as described, alternating the set-up role between all adults in the classroom. During naptime (or other planning periods built into the day), the adult who has been responsible for planning activities in the past should meet with the staff member who has limited experience in planning activities and share his or her skills. At first, the trained adult should plan activities that the adult with limited experience will be responsible for (explaining their purpose and design) and have the adult with limited experience implement them. Next, both adults should take an active role in planning the activities that the adult with limited experience is responsible for, including brainstorming ideas, getting the plan on paper, and preparing materials. The adult with limited experience should be responsible for implementing the plan. Gradually, the adult with limited experience should begin planning activities on his or her own, having the experienced adult approve them before implementation. Finally, the adult who began with limited experience will be ready to plan and implement activities without assistance. Although this strategy requires more time on the part of both adults initially, ultimately the team will benefit from sharing responsibility for activity planning among all members.

ZONE DEFENSE SCHEDULE IMPLEMENTATION CHECKLIST

A checklist can be used to ensure that the ZDS is being implemented properly in the classroom (a blank checklist can be found on page 138 in Appendix B). To complete the checklist, observe each transition during the day, one day per week (or more often, if desired). Indicate the current activity and the activity scheduled to follow it, and mark the number of staff members that are present. Next, rate to what extent the following occur:

- A schedule is posted.
- Children are given a transition warning.

- Children are allowed to make transitions at an individual pace.
- Zones are clearly defined.
- Adults are available at the old and new activity site.
- Activities are prepared.
- The new routine is appealing to children.
- The old activity is cleaned up.
- The set-up role is used for unplanned situations.
- The set-up role is alternated, both during the day and each week.
- The classroom focus is on engagement.
- Activities are of short duration.
- The ZDS is being followed.

SUMMARY

The ZDS is an effective tool for scheduling staff members in such a way that child nonengagement is limited during activities and transitions between activities. It features the assignment of one adult to the set-up role during each activity to take care of extra classroom tasks so that at least one other adult can focus solely on the scheduled activity and the engagement of the class. During transitions between activities, one adult stays at the old activity, keeping children engaged with the task until they decide to leave, and one adult waits at the new activity, ready to immediately involve children in the task when they arrive. The ZDS helps to limit opportunities for children to become nonengaged throughout their day. It also helps to empower classroom staff by ensuring that each adult in the classroom is responsible for planning and leading activities at some point.

Discussion Questions

1. What are the duties of the adult in the set-up role?
2. What is the focus of the adult leading the scheduled activity?
3. How are activity zones staffed during transitions? What is the purpose of this type of staffing?
4. Define *nonengagement*. How does the ZDS limit nonengagement?
5. How does your classroom staff currently manage transitions between activities?
6. How does your classroom staff currently coordinate roles and plan activities?
7. What roles are currently being fulfilled by each staff member in your classroom, and why? What gaps exist in the children's progression through daily activities as a result of the roles served by classroom staff?
8. How might using the ZDS benefit your classroom?

Notes and Ideas

Section III

Strategies for Improving Engagement in Individual Children

The Routines-Based Interview

- The Routines-Based Interview is a method for gathering information about a child and family's daily activities and intervention priorities.
- Gathering information about daily routines provides information about what a child is able to do and what skills a child needs to learn to function better in everyday contexts.
- The Routines-Based Interview allows parents and teachers to give each other information so teams can make decisions with complete information.
- As part of the Routines-Based Interview, families take responsibility for determining outcomes and prioritizing them.

WHAT IS THE ROUTINES-BASED INTERVIEW?

The Routines-Based Interview (RBI; McWilliam, 2005a) is a method for collecting information about a child's daily activities in order to develop a functional intervention plan. The child's caregivers are interviewed to collect information about the family's activities from the time the first person wakes up in the morning to the time he or she goes to bed. Parents and teachers are both interviewed to get an accurate view of the child's environments and how the child responds to those environments. Information is gathered about what everyone else does during the routine, what the child does, how the child participates, how independent the child is, if the child interacts with peers or adults, and the family's satisfaction with the routine (or teacher's impression of the goodness of fit between the child and routine). The hallmarks of the RBI are its family centeredness, focus on routines, and focus on functional domains.

Family Centeredness

The RBI is a family-centered method for intervention planning because of the input the family has and the relationship that the method creates between the family and program beginning on the initial visit. When the family enters the program, the first thing the family members do is talk with their child's prospective teacher and other staff about their child. This is the family's chance to show their expertise about their child and his or her development. Families enjoy the RBI process because it concerns everyone in the family, not just the child in early intervention, and they feel gratified that someone is interested in hearing about their daily life. Whereas communication with families often does not begin until the initiation of services and implementation of the intervention plan, using the RBI creates an open flow of communication from planning onward.

In addition, the RBI is family-centered because of the family's active role in providing information and selecting and prioritizing outcomes. The RBI is a time for professionals to gather information—not to make suggestions. Families are encouraged to speak freely because they know they are not being judged, there are no right or wrong answers, and they do not need to impress anyone. Family members are the experts on the child because professionals do not have an accurate view of daily life in the family, even if they make frequent home visits. At the end of the interview, the family selects the priorities they would like to focus on. They then put the outcomes in priority order, and this becomes the intervention plan for the child's team.

Focus on Routines

Routines are merely times of the day. Every family has them, no matter how chaotic life may be. Routines are not necessarily scheduled; they are activities that happen on a fairly frequent basis. For instance, home routines include waking up, eating breakfast, getting dressed, eating dinner, taking a bath, and going to bed. They can even include activities such as going to church, going to a Mother's Day Out program once a week, visiting grandparents on the weekend, and making a monthly trip to the doctor's office. Classroom routines include activities such as arrival, free play, circle time, snack, outside play, art, centers, nap, lunch, and departure.

The RBI is structured around routines because they make sense to families—daily events are organized sequentially by routine. Without preparing or taking data, a family can easily report on a typical day and how the child is able to function in each routine. Family members also know, without having to put too much thought into it, whether they are satisfied with their routines. Organizing an interview around routines empowers the family because it gives family members a chance to share information about their child in an organized way.

Focus on Functional Domains

During the RBI, families (and teachers) are asked to report on the child's engagement, independence, and social relationships within each routine. These domains are the focus of the interview because they are functional—they promote child success in the current environment. Traditional domains such as fine motor, gross motor, self-help, communication, and cognition are not ignored; they are embedded within the functional domains. For instance, information about the child's communication skills will be revealed when information is gathered about the child's interactions in routines. Likewise, information about fine and gross motor skills and self-help skills will be obtained when the family and teacher report on how independently the child can complete a given routine. Focusing on engagement, independence, and social relationships instead of the traditional domains increases the chances that outcomes will be functional (useful and clear) for families. For instance, the necessity in having a child's speech be understood is clear (functional focus on social relationships), whereas the necessity in having a child produce bilabial sounds may not be well understood by families (nonfunctional focus on communication).

HOW DO I CONDUCT A ROUTINES-BASED INTERVIEW?

There are a few general tips to know about the structure of the RBI before delving into the details of the interview. Most important, the RBI is not a structured, standardized interview. It should feel like an informal conversation and feel comfortable for the family. In fact, the RBI has considerable structure, but that structure is hidden from the family in the interest of making it conversational. The interviewer does not need to ask a specific list of questions; each interview will be different depending on the family. The interviewer merely needs to ask enough questions to get a good feel for the family's routines and the family's concerns and satisfaction with each. It is also important to remember that the interviewer guides the conversation and listens to the family; he or she does not make suggestions. Suggestions may cause the family to feel as if they are being judged—as if there are right and wrong answers to the questions. The purpose of the RBI is to provide a structure for families to openly share information about their routines and their child; judgment is not part of the process.

It is best to interview the family and the child's teacher at the same time, if this can be arranged. Including the teacher in the RBI gives the family accurate information about the child's classroom behavior, which the family can use to help make decisions about intervention. In addition, including both the family and teacher in the interview highlights the importance of input from all caregivers. When the teacher is meaningfully included in intervention planning, implementation is more likely to occur because the teacher, as well as the family, owns the goals. When both the family and teacher are involved in the RBI, the family should be interviewed first about all daily home and community routines. The teacher is interviewed second and reports on all classroom routines.

Any member of the intervention team with appropriate interpersonal skills can conduct the interview. The key is for the interviewer to relax and not ask a checklist of questions. The interviewer should show genuine interest in the family, empathize with them, and accept their decisions. The family should feel comfortable talking to the interviewer and sharing information about home and community activities. Initially, it may be easier to have one person conduct the interview while another person takes notes. This does not necessarily mean that two staff members are needed; if the teacher is being interviewed as part of the RBI process, he or she could take notes while the family reports on home and community routines, leaving the interviewer responsible for taking notes only while the teacher reports on classroom routines.

With these general considerations in mind, we present the details of the RBI process. There are six general steps to the process.

The Interviewer Prepares the Family to Report on Daily Routines

It is important to prepare families for the RBI so they understand why they are being asked to discuss home and community activities. The family should be told that the interviewer is interested in learning about family members' priorities for themselves and the child and that the preferred way of learning about those priorities is by hearing what daily life is like for them. It may be helpful for some families to complete a Family Preparation Form before the interview. The Family Preparation Form briefly explains the purpose of the meeting and provides families with a structure for thinking about their daily activities and concerns they wish to address. (A blank form can be found on pages 139–141 in Appendix B.) The Family Preparation Form should be given to all families, although completion of the form should not be required.

Another part of preparing the family for the RBI is keeping the entire process, from planning and scheduling onward, family centered. In other words, the family should be asked about their preferences regarding who will attend the interview, where it will take place, and when it will occur. Family members may have as few or as many caregivers as they would like to be present to share information about the child.

The Family Reports on Daily Routines

At the beginning of the RBI, it is a good idea to remind families about the purpose of the meeting and the structure chosen. Although this does not have to be repeated verbatim, an example of a way to begin the interview is by saying,

> To come up with a plan for helping you and your child, I'd like to ask you about your day-to-day life. By talking about what you normally do, you will be in a good position to pick the things that are most important to your family, including your child. By focusing on the day-to-day things, we can make our suggestions fit with what your child and family are already doing.

Before beginning, the interviewer should ask family members if they have any concerns or questions. The family should be assured that concerns about particular routines will be addressed as those routines are discussed.

It is best to go through the family's routines in sequential order. Therefore, an easy way to start the interview is by asking the family, "How does your day start?" Note that this question addresses how the day starts for the first person awake, and this might not necessarily be the child. Many parents will begin by talking about how their child wakes up, but with further probing the interviewer might find out that one or both parents have already been awake for a while, taking care of household tasks. An easy way to move the questioning from one routine to another is to ask, "Then what happens?" or "What's next?"

As family members talk about each routine, the interviewer should ask questions to gather information about six key areas: what everyone in the family does during the routine, what the child does during the routine, how the child participates in the routine, what the child does by him- or herself, how the child communicates and gets along with others during the routine, and how satisfied family members are with the routine (see Table 5.1). It is important to ask the family about satisfaction with routines because each family has a unique environment and unique expectations for that environment. This information gives the interviewer an idea of the family's perceived quality of life. An interviewer might think a family's routine sounds chaotic but then find out that the family is satisfied with it; on the other hand, the interviewer might think a routine sounds fine but then find out the family is dissatisfied with it and would like to make changes.

Table 5.1. Key questions to ask about each family routine

What does everyone do during this time?
What does the child do?
How does the child participate in the routine?
What does the child do by him- or herself?
How does the child communicate and get along with other family members during this routine?
How satisfied are you with the routine?

The Teacher Reports on Classroom Routines

After the family has reported on home and community routines, the teacher reports on classroom routines. As with the family's part of the interview, the teacher should go through the day in sequential order, from arrival to departure. For each routine, the interviewer should ask questions to gather information about what all of the children do during the activity, what the child being discussed does, the child's engagement, the child's independence, the child's social relationships, and the goodness of fit between the routine and the child. To prepare to report on these things, the teacher should know the classroom schedule and become familiar with the child's level of engagement, independence, and social relationships in each classroom routine prior to the interview.

The Interviewer Reviews Strengths and Concerns

After both the family and teacher have reported about the child's daily activities, the interviewer should review the strengths, concerns, and possible intervention areas brought up during the interview. This helps to refresh the family's memory about everything they have said and to review the concerns that were addressed. It is a good idea to star important items in the notes as they come up during the interview. This makes it easier to go back and review important information that was given. The interviewer can give the family the notes taken during the interview so they can look over them. This shows the family that the interviewer has no secrets and was not making any judgments during the interview. It also gives the family a chance to see possible intervention areas (the starred items) instead of just hearing about them. Making sure the family has a good understanding of the information is important because after reviewing strengths and concerns the interviewer asks the family to consider the areas discussed and think about the areas that the intervention team should focus on. It is the family's role to suggest intervention areas.

The Family Selects Outcomes

After reviewing the starred items on the interviewer's notes and considering the information shared by the teacher, the family can begin to choose potential intervention areas. For instance, a family member might say, "Dinner preparation time really needs to be on the list. Like I said before, I don't have enough hands to make dinner, help the older children with their homework, entertain Evelyn, and deal with phone calls and doorbells ringing!" The interviewer can ask clarifying questions to determine that the family is interested in two outcomes: 1) having the oldest sibling help the middle child with his homework and 2) teaching 36-month-old Evelyn to play with toys for longer periods of time. In this way, the family's suggestions about intervention areas become the outcomes for the child and family. The interviewer records these outcomes in the family's words so they reflect exactly what the family hopes for. It is typical for families to come up with between 6 and 10 outcomes.

The Family Prioritizes the Outcomes

The last step in the RBI process is to have the family prioritize the outcomes they have generated. The family is shown the list of outcomes and asked to put them in order of importance. From this point forward, the outcomes will always be listed in the family's priority order.

TOOLS FOR CONDUCTING A ROUTINES-BASED INTERVIEW

Being comfortable with the RBI process takes time and practice. Some tools to help interviewers learn the process and assess their implementation of the procedure are found on pages 154–155 in Appendix B. The RBI Report Form (see pages 142–153 of Appendix B) can be used to take notes during the interview and list a family's outcomes. It reminds the interviewer to ask about key areas (engagement, independence, and social relationships) and gather information about the family's satisfaction with each routine. The second page of the form can be copied multiple times for recording information for each routine discussed. At the end of the form, examples of questions that can be asked about each routine are listed, although it should be noted that the RBI is a conversation and asking a list of specific questions is not recommended. After the interview, the RBI Implementation Checklist can be completed to ensure that the appropriate procedure was followed in scheduling the interview, conducting it, and planning interventions.

DESMOND IS 4 YEARS OLD, loves his dog, Maggie, which he calls "Aggie," and attends a classroom program in which a majority of the children do not have disabilities but some do. His classroom teacher, Sandy, is a skilled, sensitive teacher who provides Desmond with many learning opportunities. This is an excerpt from an RBI with Sandy and Desmond's mother, Renée, in which Renée describes getting ready for the day.

Interviewer: So where is Desmond when you go into your room to get dressed and so on?

Renée: I can leave him in the den.

Interviewer: As far as you know, what does he do in there? [looking for a description of Desmond's behavior during this routine]

Renée: That's the problem. He doesn't do anything.

Interviewer: Nothing at all? He just sits there?

Renée: Yes. I put the TV on but he seems to ignore it. His toys are in a basket next to the fireplace, but they're untouched when I come back.

Interviewer: How long is that? [seeking information about Desmond's engagement]

Renée: Fifteen, maybe twenty minutes.

Interviewer: By this time, Dan [Desmond's father] is gone, right? [finding out what everyone else is doing]

Renée: Right.

Interviewer: Okay, so Desmond sits in the den, where he has things that could entertain him but he just sits there doing nothing. Right? [using active listening techniques]

Renée: Right.

Interviewer: How do you feel about this? [beginning to find out the mother's satisfaction with this routine]

Renée: Part of me is relieved. I know he's not getting into trouble. He used to climb on the furniture. But part of me feels guilty. A child shouldn't be so inactive.

Interviewer: Okay, so on a scale of 1 to 5, how happy are you with this time of day? [asking about family satisfaction]

Renée: About a 3.

Interviewer: Then what happens, after you're dressed? [This is how the next routine is identified, allowing the family to inform the interviewer what routines occur.]

Renée: Then it's time to leave for school.

Interviewer: How does that go?

Renée: Terrible. As soon as I start trying to get him to get ready, he starts fighting me.
Interviewer: What do you mean "fighting" you? [Follow-up questions are usually asked to elicit either behavioral descriptions or evaluative statements; this is the former.]
Renée: First, he covers his ears and says, "No, no, no," over and over.
Interviewer: How do you handle that?
Renée: I have no option. I'm like, "Desmond, don't start in on me with that mess. We have to go to school, just like every other day."
Interviewer: How do you get him out of the house then?
Renée: Oh, we go through a lot before we get near the door. As soon as I get near him to take him by the hand, he hits at me, kicks at me. Sometimes runs away.
Interviewer: And you keep after him, I guess, because you really do have to leave.
Renée: I act like I do! Anyways, that's what I do, I chase after him or hold his arm or leg so he can't get at me.
Interviewer: So you basically have no choice but to manhandle him out of the house?
Renée: Right, and then you should see me trying to get the car door open, him in his car seat, and the belts on.

After a few more detailed questions, the interviewer wraps up the questioning about this routine.

Interviewer: This doesn't sound like much fun. On a scale of 1 to 5, how would you rate this getting-out-of-the-house time?
Renée: Can I go lower than 1?

A little later in the interview, they discuss dinner time.

Renée: This is his best time of day. He loves to eat.
Interviewer: Does he sit in a regular chair?
Renée: Yes, on a phone book on a regular chair.
Interviewer: Is Dan home at this time? [finding out what everyone else is doing]
Renée: Yes, usually the three of us eat together.
Interviewer: And how is this Desmond's best time? [eliciting a behavioral description]
Renée: He eats good. He's kinda slow, but that's good. That gives me and Dan time to talk.
Interviewer: Good. That's important. And Desmond eats fine with his fork? [giving affirmation to encourage the mother to continue]
Renée: Oh, yes. He can even cut lots of things with a knife. He's really good with his knife, fork, and spoon.
Interviewer: And drinking?
Renée: You mean, is he an alcoholic?
Interviewer: No—
Renée: Just kidding. I know what you're asking. He drinks fine from a regular cup.
Interviewer: So it sounds as though things go well at dinnertime. What do you think Desmond will be able to do next that he's not doing now? [When all is well in a routine, asking what the family expects the child to be able to do next is a positive way of obtaining a goal for the routine.]
Renée: What do you mean?
Interviewer: For example, does he talk to you much at dinner?
Renée: No. He's busy eating and, like I said before, he doesn't talk much.
Interviewer: So is that something you expect to see him be able to do more of at dinner?
Renée: It would be nice. I feel bad that me and Dan kind of ignore him because he's so good at dinner. [The interviewer has elicited this possible outcome; it remains to be seen whether Renée will choose it. Choosing outcomes occurs after the interviewing is over. Interviewers need to be ethical in what they elicit and how. In this case, Renée was given the opportunity to identify her own next step. Like many parents, however, she needed some information. The interviewer's example was not based on what Desmond should already be doing but rather on what would come next developmentally.]
Interviewer: On a scale of 1 to 5, how well do you feel dinner is going?
Renée: About a 5.

The following part of the RBI describes what Sandy, the teacher, reports about classroom routines.

Interviewer: You said the first routine of the day is arrival. What goes on at arrival? [asking what the norm for the routine is—what everyone else does]
Sandy: Parents bring their children to the room, talk to us, sign in, put lunches away, and so on.
Interviewer: What do the children do?
Sandy: They have free play.
Interviewer: And Desmond? How does he do with this early-morning free play? [asking what this child does]
Sandy: If we're free to sit down and do something with him, he does okay for a little while. But if we're talking to parents or playing with other children, he tends not to go get engaged with toys.
Interviewer: What does he do?
Sandy: He kinda wanders around.
Interviewer: Does he watch other kids or adults playing or does he just sort of—? [asking about engagement with peers and adults, which is also about social relationships]
Sandy: He just wanders without really paying attention to anything.
Interviewer: How long will this go on?
Sandy: It can go on for 15 minutes if we don't get him going with some toy or something.
Interviewer: On a scale of 1 to 5, how well do you think free play is working for Desmond? [When interviewing the teacher, the interviewer phrases the question in terms of the goodness of fit between the routine and the child.]
Sandy: Like a 1. He needs more structure.

Later in the interview, Sandy talks about center time.

Interviewer: What happens at center time?
Sandy: We set up about four stations or centers that have something to do with the theme of the month. Usually, one center has art supplies, another has books, another has small toys, and another has a teacher-led activity. The kids often choose the teacher-led activity.
Interviewer: What about Desmond?
Sandy: He sort of hangs on the periphery. If I try to call him into the activity, he walks away. He acts as though he wants to see what's going on but doesn't want to have to do anything.
Interviewer: Is it that he doesn't want to do anything or he freaks at having to interact with other people?
Sandy: It could be that, but I can't even get him to do something by himself. He just pushes me away.
Interviewer: So, in that situation, for him to do something by himself, he'd first have to interact with you. Right? [The interviewer is testing the hypothesis that the problem might not be that Desmond does not want to do anything, which is an unobservable mental construct and one they cannot check out with Desmond himself because of his limited language. Instead, the hypothesis is that most attempts to get Desmond engaged involve a social interaction, which may be aversive to him.]
Sandy: Right.
Interviewer: What if you just leave him to his own devices?
Sandy: It would be like free time. He'd just wander around, doing nothing.
Interviewer: So does he actually go up to other kids at center time?
Sandy: He'll go near them but he doesn't initiate anything with them. And they now know him and just leave him alone. [This information reveals that if Desmond is to be engaged, some level of interaction with the teacher will be necessary.]
Interviewer: So he has little real interaction with other children during center time? On a scale from 1 to 5, how well would you say centers are working for Desmond?
Sandy: Maybe a 2. Sometimes he does go find something to do, but it's never for long.

These excerpts from the RBI are fairly typical in the amount of detail for a child receiving classroom-based services. There is not much time for very detailed descriptions about what happens, but enough to elicit concerns or potential outcomes.

WHAT DO I DO IF . . . ?

What are some options for clearing 2 hours of time for staff members to participate in a Routines-Based Interview?

The professional responsible for doing the RBI needs to have 2 hours for the interview. Otherwise, the interview will be rushed and might omit important priorities. The actual interview might last only 1 to 1½ hours, but extra time is needed for conversation before and after the interview.

Teachers sometimes cannot participate in a whole interview, especially if it is at a time convenient for the family but not the teacher. In this situation, the interview is conducted with the teacher first, without the family, and the interviewer relays information about each classroom routine to the family.

What if another agency is responsible for creating the child's IFSP or IEP?

Three options are available for dealing with this situation. The first and preferred is to persuade the other agency to incorporate the RBI into its individualized family service plan (IFSP) or individualized education program (IEP) process. People who already know how to do an RBI can offer to do the interview itself, even if someone from another agency organizes the process. A second option is to conduct an RBI before the IFSP or IEP meeting, so the family can take functional outcomes or goals to the meeting. The agency not involved with the RBI, however, could object that they were not involved in the development of the list of outcomes or goals. Furthermore, it puts the onus on the family to advocate for their priorities. Another disadvantage of this option is that potentially key people (e.g., those at the non–RBI agency) would have missed hearing about the functional needs, which are discussed during the RBI. A third option is to do an RBI after the IFSP or IEP has been developed. This creates a "shadow plan"—a functional plan, agreed on by team members, that is in addition to the nonfunctional plan on the legal documents that fulfill agency requirements—from which outcomes are addressed. Obviously, this is not a good situation, especially if the two plans are incongruous. Services would be designed to match the actual IFSP or IEP rather than the shadow plan. This option should only be used if 1) the agency responsible for the IFSP or IEP is unwilling to incorporate the RBI into the process or 2) the RBI cannot be done (or the agency refuses to look at the outcomes developed during an RBI) before the IFSP or IEP is done.

What if the family does not give me information?

The responsibility for this situation lies with the interviewer, who can do the following:

- Examine whether interview skills can be improved or whether another person might be better suited for interviewing this family. Sometimes, communication failures are the result of a lack of trust, which can sometimes be overcome by using a different approach.
- Ask the family if there is something else they want to talk about. It could be that the focus on routines is irrelevant to the family's current concerns. Generally, however, an RBI will provide enough of an opportunity for the family to talk about whatever else is on their mind.
- Ask the family what they expect the child to be able to do next. If the family does not provide information during the RBI, it might be because they do not perceive anything to be wrong. Focusing on what the child might be able to do next is a more proactive approach than identifying problems.

What if the family only wants to talk about services?

The family can be told politely that services cannot be discussed until everyone knows what they are for, so the first step is to identify needs. If the family says, for example, "I just want to make sure my child gets speech therapy," the response can be, "That might be necessary, but first we have to identify what your child needs to learn. After that, we can decide what services would get us there. And the way to identify what your child needs to learn is to go through his daily routines."

What if the family chooses an outcome as a priority that I don't think should be on the intervention plan?

One tactic would be to ask the family what made them identify this particular outcome, although if it were a functional need and the interview had gone well, the interviewer would know why the family identified it. Another tactic would be to ask the family for what routines that outcome would be helpful. This can provide context for (i.e., make functional) an outcome that might have been plucked from a developmental checklist after another professional told the family that the child lagged behind in certain areas. Asking this question might also help the family realize that the outcome actually would not help the child function better in everyday routines and therefore might not be that functional. (Functional outcomes and goals are discussed in Chapter 6.) It is important to remember, however, that the interviewer's opinion about what should be on the intervention plan is largely irrelevant. Although legally the team develops the IFSP or IEP, philosophically the IFSP or IEP should reflect the family's—not professionals'—priorities.

SUMMARY

The Routines-Based Interview is a family-friendly method for gathering information about a child's daily activities. After preparing to report on daily routines, the family shares information about what everyone in the family does during activities and about the engagement, independence, and social relationships of the child. In addition, the family's satisfaction with each routine is taken into account. After the family has reported on home and community routines, the teacher reports on classroom routines. Concerns and possible intervention areas are reviewed, and the family selects and prioritizes outcomes. The RBI results in a functional intervention plan for the child and family.

Discussion Questions

1. After you have practiced conducting the RBI, answer the following questions.
    a. Were you comfortable?
    b. What was the most difficult part of the interview?
    c. Did it feel like an informal conversation?
    d. How long did it take?
    e. How many outcomes did the family come up with?
2. How can your program use the RBI during the intake and IFSP/IEP development process?
3. What are the barriers to using the RBI, and how can you overcome them?

Notes and Ideas

Chapter 6

Developing Functional Outcomes and Goals

Key Points

- Functional goals promote child or family success in the current environment and, to some extent, in future environments.
- Functional goals address the development of the child's skills in the home, classroom, and community.
- Functional goals can be addressed by multiple people at multiple times of the day, during normal routines.

WHAT ARE FUNCTIONAL GOALS?

There are two main methods for writing goals: a developmentally based approach and a functional approach. The developmental approach is based on a model of typical development, and the purpose is to identify areas in which a child is lagging in skill development. This approach promotes the identification and correction of deficits. In contrast, a functional approach addresses the development of the child's skills in the home, classroom, and community. This approach promotes the success of the child (and family) in the current environment and in future environments. Therefore, a functional approach is individualized and strengths based rather than deficit based, as is a developmental approach.

With a functional approach, standardized test results and developmental checklists are not appropriate for developing individualized intervention plans because they do not take into account the child's context. A functional approach uses a child's daily routines as a means of assessment and allows professionals to understand what activities the child is frequently involved in, what the child is able to do in those activities, and what skills the child needs to learn to participate in the activity even more fully. Functional goals, then, reflect real-life situations and the priorities of the family (not the professionals).

WHY FOCUS ON FUNCTIONALITY?

Functional goals are important because they focus on promoting the child's success in typical, everyday activities. The child will have more opportunities to learn and practice the skill and then maintain its use in the original activity and new ones if the skill is necessary for the child to participate in daily activities. Functional goals are easy to address because the context in which they can be used comes up frequently in the course of a child's typical day. In other words, functional goals are useful and meaningful to the child and family.

The true test of functionality is to ask why the child is working on the given goal. If the goal is functional, the answer should be immediately apparent. For instance, the child may need to use a thumb and finger to pick up cereal so he can feed himself or walk 10 steps with a walker so he can gain access to the playground and his peers.

More Opportunities for Practice

Functional goals can be frequently and easily addressed because they occur within the child's daily routines. The opportunity for intervention will naturally occur, so there is no need for parents, teachers, and other caregivers to create artificial situations in which the child can practice a skill. The child comes across multiple opportunities to use the needed skill throughout his or her day and therefore multiple opportunities to practice the skill. In addition, functional goals are written in plain language so they can be understood by anyone; therefore, different people can address the child's goals at several times during the day, during normal routines and activities.

Immediately Useful

Functional goals focus on engagement, independence, and social relationships. These domains are useful in a child's daily contexts, so the child can work on being successful in current daily routines rather than focusing on skills that will only be helpful in the future. Furthermore, because functional goals are based on family priorities gathered during the RBI, team members know that there is a contextual need for the skills the child is working on—if there were not, the skills would not have come up during the interview.

These alternative domains or outcomes—engagement, independence, and social relationships (McWilliam, 2005c)—are exhaustive and not mutually exclusive. This means that they cover all areas of children's daily functioning and that they overlap. They have the advantage over traditional test domains of not being associated with disciplines. Therefore, all specialists can contribute to children's daily functioning in any of these alternative domains. Perhaps more significantly, difficulties in any of the alternative domains during given routines do not automatically indicate the need for specific services. This lack of alignment helps the decision-making about services to be more thoughtful and less automatic (and less flawed).

Renée (the parent profiled in the RBI in Chapter 5) chose the following goals for her son, Desmond. They are not worded formally; this is how they were written down at the goal-selection stage of the RBI.

1. Initiate play with toys, especially in the morning when Renée is dressing and during arrival time at school.
2. Getting out of the house in the morning without throwing a fit.
3. Talk at dinnertime.
4. Join other children during free-choice times, such as centers.

Typically, families choose 6–10 goals. The four listed here are based on the short excerpts from the RBI provided in Chapter 5.

HOW DO I WRITE A FUNCTIONAL GOAL?

When preparing to write an IFSP or IEP, remember that functional goals do not come from standardized tests. Instead, functional goals are created after talking to families about their priorities (i.e., after completing an RBI). The intervention document is created after talking with families in a semi-structured way and is a direct reflection of the family's priorities. The goal statement may need to be reworded, but the purpose of the goal should reflect the family's wishes. Using family priorities to create goals results in an intervention plan that is practical (feasible for the caregivers to work on during daily routines) and that addresses skills the child will be able to use immediately (increasing success and independence in daily routines).

Team members should consider the breadth and specificity of each goal. If a goal is so broad that a caregiver could do almost anything with it, it will not be useful in guiding intervention. On the other hand, if a goal is so specific that it does not allow for generalization, it will not be useful because it will not be functional. The main categories that should be addressed when writing a goal are necessity, context, learning stage, and criteria.

Necessity

A skill can be considered necessary if a child would not be able to be engaged without having it. For example, if the child cannot hold a spoon, his or her engagement at meals is compromised. The child might be able to participate at some level without the skill, but the sophistication of eating would be attenuated. So the necessity of a target behavior is defined by the fact that the behavior facilitates engagement.

Goals betraying a lack of necessity reflect skills that are atypical for typically developing children. For example, *Child will blow through a straw successfully on 5 of 7 trials* describes a behavior that a typically developing child would not do. Another unnecessary kind of goal is the one that might be a normally occurring skill but that is not needed in everyday life. These skills often show up on developmental checklists or as part of curricula. For example, *Child will main-*

tain kneeling for 20 seconds can occur in typically developing children, but is it necessary for children to have this target behavior? Professionals can fall into the trap of believing that precursor skills are necessary for development. For example, early infant crawling has been determined by some researchers to predict later motor skill development (McEwan, Dihoff, & Brosvic, 1991). This information might lead to a goal for crawling, yet a number of typically developing infants do not crawl. They scoot on their bottoms, roll, or go directly to walking. Early interventionists might mistakenly focus specifically on crawling rather than on independent movement. This is the difference between a strict developmental approach (believing that children must go through a developmental sequence) and a functional approach (helping children participate, be independent, and have social relationships).

Context

It is also important to consider the context in which a behavior or skill will be useful. Goal statements should include information about the routine or routines in which the goal could or should be addressed. For instance, a goal statement might specify that a child will use his or her thumb and finger to pick up small objects and put them in a basket during cleanup time at home and school. Specifying the routine in which the goal should be addressed gives caregivers guidance about when to provide intervention. In this example, caregivers could teach the child to use the thumb and finger to feed him- or herself during meals, but what was determined to be necessary was picking up small objects at cleanup time, so that would be stated in the goal. Working on finger-feeding would be a *strategy* toward accomplishing the goal.

Context can also be an important factor in measuring the achievement of a goal. Instead of adding a meaningless criterion to the end of a goal statement, team members should think about what makes sense for determining when a child is ready to move from learning one skill to the next. The key to coming up with logical criteria is matching a criterion to the purpose of the goal. If a child's goal is to say "I want to play" to join peers on the playground, measuring the acquisition of the goal by assessing the child's vocabulary in a speech-language pathologist's office is inappropriate. The child should be assessed on the playground in the presence of peers to see if he or she has acquired the skill in a typical and useful context.

Occasionally, goals are written for professionals rather than for children or families. For instance, the statement *Physical therapy will be provided once a week to help Emma walk independently* is not a functional goal statement. Goals should be written for children, not for their therapists or teachers. (IFSPs and IEPs can include goals written for parents.) Changing the statement to *Emma will walk by herself from the living room to the kitchen for dinner* is more functional and implies that Emma will have an active role in her intervention.

Learning Stage

Functional goals reflect which one or more of the four stages of learning is being addressed: acquisition, generalization, fluency, and maintenance. This will generally be included in the criteria, as described in the following section. In the acquisition stage, a child first learns a skill; generalization refers to the child's use of the skill across situations. Functional programming often involves working on both of these stages at the same time, which is known as programming for generalization (Stokes & Baer, 1977). Fluency is the ability to perform the skill at such a rate or with enough ease and smoothness to allow a child to succeed in a routine (e.g., *walk fast enough to keep up with peers, speak clearly and quickly enough that others wait*). Another stage is maintenance, which means that the skill is sustained and does not go away. A functional goal is clear about what stage or stages are being addressed.

Criteria

The purpose of criteria is to let the team, including the family, know when the goal has been accomplished. Without measurable criteria, there is ambiguity. Although some IFSP and IEP documents repeatedly specify that a skill will occur 80% of the time, there are actually many ways to measure acquisition, generalization, fluency, and maintenance. In addition to the percentage of time in which a child displays a behavior or skill, which requires data collection about the total time available and the total time spent displaying the target behavior or skill, acquisition can be measured in the following ways:

- Identifying the proportion of opportunities in which the child demonstrates the behavior or skill (e.g., 3 of 5 opportunities)
- Identifying the percentage of accuracy with which the child demonstrates the behavior or skill (e.g., 8 of 10 correct)
- Using time sampling (e.g., one time per day)
- Identifying the absolute number (e.g., with two peers)
- Judging the extent of the child's independence (e.g., with only a little help)

Some of the strategies used to measure acquisition can also be used to measure generalization, maintenance, and fluency. Generalization can be measured by

- Routines (e.g., during circle time, snack, and outside)
- People (e.g., with Mom, Dad, and Grandma)
- Materials (e.g., when playing with three different toys)
- Places (e.g., at storytime, at the swimming pool, at the cafeteria)

Fluency can be measured by considering duration (e.g., for 2 minutes, in no more than 5 minutes, keeping pace with other children) or quality (e.g., smoothly, with ease, controlled). Maintenance can be measured using

- Time sampling (e.g., for 2 months)
- The degree of independence displayed (e.g., without help)
- The absolute number (e.g., during five trips to the library)

Additional Tips

When writing goals, some verbs are more functional than others. For instance, *point* and *say* are functional, whereas *improve* and *identify* are not. What is the difference? Functional verbs refer to actions that can be observed. A parent can ask a teacher if the action occurred, and the teacher can easily give a yes or no answer. A teacher can see a child point to her name and immediately know that the goal was achieved; the child can say "more juice" and the teacher immediately knows that the child used a two-word phrase to make a request. Other examples of functional verbs include *write, name, share, sing,* and *put away,* just to name a few.

Nonfunctional verbs are not measurable and should be avoided. For instance, if a child's goal is to improve his communication skills, how do the parent and teacher know when the goal has been achieved? How much does the child need to improve in order to have met the goal? Likewise, if a child's goal is to identify his or her name, has the goal been met when the child points to it, says it, picks up a card with the correct name on it, or puts his or her coat on the appropriately labeled hook? Other examples of verbs that indicate hard-to-measure goals include *understand* (how would this be measured?), *exhibit* (by saying, pointing, matching, or following directions without help?), and *increase* (by 1 word or step, or by 10 words or steps?). Changing a verb from nonfunctional to functional involves asking what the behavior should look like. For instance, instead of *become involved in circle time* (nonfunctional), the goal could be written as *Suzie will stay in circle time for 3 minutes to choose a song from the choice board and sing it with her peers* (functional).

In addition to choosing functional verbs, professionals should also avoid using jargon when writing a goal. Remember, goals should be clear and easily understood by a variety of people across different settings so the child can practice the skill in any daily routine. The easiest way to avoid using jargon is to write down the family's priority using their words. The priority might need to be reworded when it is formed into a goal, but as much of the family's wording as possible should remain as part of the goal. To distinguish between jargon and clear terms, team members can ask themselves if the family would describe the goal in the same words. For instance, would a mother tell a babysitter that Riley needs to ambulate 3 feet in his walker? Probably not. Instead, the mother would tell the babysitter that Riley is learning to take five steps with his walker to get the toy he wants to play with. Likewise, a mother is likely to tell a babysitter that Riley is learning to use his thumb and finger to pick up food rather than saying that he should use a pincer grasp at mealtime. Instead of telling the babysitter to give Riley minimal physical assistance, the mother would tell the babysitter to give him only a little bit of help.

Finally, it is a good idea to assess goals to ensure that they are functional. The Goal Functionality Scale II (McWilliam, 2005d) can be used to score goals based on their functionality. To use the scale, a goal is assigned a score of 3, 4, or 5 based on its usefulness. Next, points are added for functional items or subtracted for nonfunctional items. The resulting score yields an indication of the functionality of the goal. Goals that score between 7 and 13 are considered very functional, scores between 4 and 7 indicate fairly functional goals, and scores between 0 and 3 suggest that goals are nonfunctional. (A blank form of the scale can be found on page 156 of Appendix B.)

Annabel has written the following goal and assesses it with the Goal Functionality Scale II:

> Gabby will participate in mealtimes, car rides, and bed time by speaking clearly. We will know she can do this when she says five things ("turns") in a conversation that her mother or father can understand—at one mealtime, during one car ride, and at one bedtime in one week.

See Figure 6.1 for Annabel's completed Goal Functionality Scale II form. This was the fifth priority in Gabby's family's list of goals, so it is goal number 5. Of the traditional domains, it addresses communication. Speaking in an understandable way—what some people would call an "articulation goal"—is generally useful, so it receives a starting score of 5. Note that had the goal been for Gabby to use the /sh/ sound with 80% accuracy, the usefulness score would have been 4 (*not really useful*), because saying "sh" out of context, for no reason, or for a therapist is not a useful skill. Annabel was able to add one point because her goal did address pragmatic communication, which is part of social relationships (SR). She added another point because the goal also addressed naturalistic social interaction—another SR goal. Although understandability is important for developing friendships, this outcome does not address friendship development specifically. It does receive one more point for addressing participation. In fact, in our work we now begin almost all child-level outcomes with *[child] will participate in [list routines] by [performing the skill the family has chosen to work on]*. Annabel's goal has reached a score of 8 to this point. It is a good goal and none of the subtraction items apply, so the total score stands at 8. Annabel has heard that we consider goals of 5–6 to be good, so she is pleased and proceeds to incorporate it into Gabby's IFSP.

Goal Functionality Scale II

		Domain (circle one):	
Child's name/ID:	*Gabby*	Cognitive	Social-emotional
Goal/objective #:	5	(Communication)	Adaptive
Rater's initials:	*Annabel*	Motor	

1. Is this goal GENERALLY USEFUL (i.e., can you answer *why* and *who cares*; broad enough yet specific enough)? If YES,	(5)
2. ...NOT REALLY USEFUL? If YES,	4
3. ...NOT AT ALL USEFUL? If YES,	3

4. Addresses **duration** of interaction with people or objects (E)	+1	12. Cannot tell in what normalized **contexts** it would be useful	–1
5. Persistence (E)	+1	13. Purpose is not evident or useful	–1
6. Developmentally and contextually appropriate **construction** (E)	+1	14. Some element makes little sense	–1
7. Pragmatic **communication** (SR)	(+1)	15. Unnecessary skill	–1
8. Naturalistic **social interaction** (SR)	(+1)	16. Jargon	–1
9. **Friendship** (SR)	+1	17. Increase/decrease	–1
10. Developmentally appropriate **independence** in routines (not just a reflection of prompt level) (I)	+1	18. Vague	–1
11. **Participation** in developmentally appropriate activities (E)	(+1)	19. Insufficient criterion	–1
SCORE	*8*	20. Criterion present but does not reflect a useful level of behavior	–1

Figure 6.1. Goal Functionality Scale II filled out for Gabby.

WHAT DO I DO IF . . . ?

What if my school district forces me to put academic goals or state learning standards on a child's intervention plan? How do you write a functional academic goal?

The best solution is to conduct an RBI, as described in Chapter 5, and then identify which academic goals or state standards align with the goals that emerge from the interview. This might require stretching the definition of alignment. The problem with the requirement to have such goals on a plan is that it misconstrues the purpose of the IEP. The Individuals with Disabilities Education Improvement Act (IDEIA) of 2004 (PL 108-446) says that the IEP must include

> (II) a statement of measurable annual goals, including academic and functional goals, designed to—aa) meet the child's needs that result from the child's disability to enable the child to be involved in and make progress in the general education curriculum; and bb) meet each of the child's other educational needs that result from the child's disability.

It does not say that the goals should be the elements of the general education curriculum. The IEP is supposed to address those needs that prevent involvement (i.e., engagement) in the activities that lead to the attainment of academic goals and state standards. Note that some academic goals, or at least preacademic goals, for preschoolers might be appropriate, but the majority of them will address play-oriented activities, which is where young children's learning occurs.

What do I do if the service providers presenting at the IFSP/IEP development meeting have their own agenda for the intervention plan and suggest nonfunctional goals?

In this situation, the person in charge of the plan needs to be able to work skillfully with team members. First, service providers need to be reminded that the family's priorities should be honored. At this age, children are still very much in the bosom of their family. Second, the plan needs to be functional so caregivers can address the goals in the course of regular routines; otherwise, the child does not receive enough intervention (learning opportunities). Third, it is possible that nonfunctional goals are actually strategies (whether they are functional strategies is another issue). For example, a therapist might say that a child really needs to work on muscle strength, and she might be upset that this goal has not emerged from the RBI. Yet, the RBI might have produced such goals as *the child will sit upright throughout circle time* and *the child will climb on playground equipment*—both very functional goals. Building up the child's strength would be a strategy for acquiring the functional goals. One hopes that the intervention would be play based and involve opportunities to practice sitting upright and playing on the playground, that is, that the strategy of building strength is incorporated into the child's routines. This would maximize the salience and amount of intervention (strength building).

What if the family's priorities reflect concerns with home routines and my district mandates that I only address child-level outcomes?

The law (IDEIA 2004; PL 108-446) says the following about the conduct of the evaluation:

> (2) CONDUCT OF EVALUATION.—In conducting the evaluation, the local educational agency shall—(A) use a variety of assessment tools and strategies to gather relevant functional, developmental, and academic information, including information provided by the parent, that may assist in determining—(i) whether the child is a child with a disability; and (ii) the content of the child's individualized education program, including information related to enabling the child to be involved in and progress in the general education curriculum, or, for preschool children, to participate in appropriate activities.

This does not address directly whether goals for home routines can be included. From a family developmental perspective, one would hope so. From an educational administrative perspective, schools should have to deal only with goals pertaining to the contexts in which they have contact with children.

The question raised, however, concerns preschoolers. A family-centered perspective on plan development can be maintained in several ways when the child is in a preschool program. First, remember that the location of services is not necessarily confined to classrooms; teachers might make occasional or even regular home visits, for example. This would help preschool staff to attend to goals pertaining to home routines. Second, special education and related-service staff can provide information to families that will help with home needs. Assistance does not always have to be direct. Third, home goals can be written so that they are linked to activities at school. This addresses the fear that districts may have of being held accountable for child progress on a home goal. For example, the family might want the child to sleep through the night, a goal that might even be related to the child's involvement in the general education curriculum, because the child gets tired in school if he or she has not slept well. If the IEP is written with an "in order to" phrase linked to school participation, the odds are that it will satisfy the requirements. For example, the goal related to sleeping through the night could be written with this tag: . . . ***in order*** *for Sam* ***to*** *participate in activities at school.* The school district could claim that it is accountable for Sam's participation in school activities, not his sleeping at night.

How do I write articulation goals in a functional way?

Ask yourself, why does a child need to articulate words? This is how functionality is always tested—with a *why* question. The answer is so that the child can be understood. Therefore, the function of articulation is to enable one to communicate effectively. Incidentally, the ability to say words clearly is not communication; does a tree falling in the forest make a sound if no one is there to hear it? It does not matter if the child can say words understandably in a speech therapy room, for example, if he or she cannot say those words understandably in the course of everyday routines, where he or she needs the skill. Therefore, the functional articulation goal is actually a communication goal, such as *Gina will participate in snack, circle, outside play, and free play by telling adults and children what she wants, in a way that they understand,* and criteria would be added. The goal might specify that Gina will use words, but the word *tell* would be appropriate if the family wanted her to communicate effectively in some manner, even if it was with gestures, signs, pictures, symbols, and so forth.

The final point about articulation goals is to be very careful not to make a developmental deficit out of a normal stage in speech development. Two children with the same speech patterns may receive differential treatment based on whether they are receiving special education services. A child not in special education learns to speak through trial and error, listening to models, and receiving the typical, corrective feedback adults tend to give children as they learn to pronounce words correctly. Ideally, a child at the same stage of speech but who is in special education would have the same learning opportunities. Too often, however, this child is required to do decontextualized activities for a therapist whereas the regular caregivers do *not* teach the child to speak properly because that is perceived as the therapist's job. Therefore, the second child actually receives less articulation therapy than the first one!

This very situation was brought up in a workshop we conducted as part of a study on improving engagement in preschool classrooms. We were discussing how speech goals, as opposed to language goals, were addressed in classrooms that were lucky enough to have speech-language pathologists in the room for 2 of the 4 half-days that the program ran each week. When we asked how the therapists contributed expertise to the classrooms, one teacher indicated that the therapist in her classroom worked on children's articulation by taking children to the side (i.e., the *one-on-one in classroom model;* McWilliam, 1996b). We then asked the teacher what she herself did to help the child learn to articulate words, and she said she did not work on that: The speech-language pathologist did. The children in this classroom, then, were getting *less* intervention with their articulation than if a speech pathologist had not been in the classroom. Without a speech pathologist, the teacher would take responsibility for teaching the preschoolers to say their words understandably, and the children would get more frequent and more contextually relevant intervention. The good news is that this teacher probably provided models and other learning opportunities for articulation even if the therapist did not release this role to her. Most preschool teachers do.

The four goals discussed in Chapter 5 that Renée had indicated for her son, Desmond, which were only four of perhaps six to ten goals generated from the RBI, were worded on the IEP as follows:

1. *Desmond will start playing with toys, without a prompt, in the morning when Renée is dressing or during arrival time at school, and keep playing for 5 minutes, 5 days in 1 week, to be able to entertain himself independently.*

   Comment: "Initiate" has been changed to more precise nonjargon, the context is specified, and the criteria are manifold and meaningful. The first criterion is the level of independence: The goal is stated for total independence. The second criterion is the duration, which has been inserted to ensure that the team realizes that casual interaction with a toy does not count. The third criterion is the rate (5 days in 1 week), which ensures that the skill is counted over days. The context is provided, which automatically makes it somewhat functional. It also raises the issue that some of these goals are for home performance, which might prompt preschool programs to question what they have to do with the child's performance in inclusive environments. Because family members are very influential in children's early education, however, it is vital that schools support families' needs that might emerge through an RBI.

2. *Desmond will leave the house for school, without becoming upset, on 3 consecutive days, so he and Renée can have a good start to their days.*

   Comment: This is another family-setting goal. If Desmond had had similar problems at school, school contexts also would have been included. This goal has implications for strategies. As currently worded, the school will help Renée through informational and emotional support. It might be possible that the school district would provide home visits for this situation, but many districts would not provide both home- and classroom-based visits in a situation such as this. In this goal statement, the undesired behavior is explicit, but the desired behavior is the focus. In their quest to be positive, sometimes professionals will skirt around the undesired behavior. This is a problem because the reader of the IEP has a hard time understanding the purpose of the goal. Functional goals have the purpose stated through a phrase beginning with *(in order) to, so (that),* and so forth.

3. *Desmond will have two "turns" as part of three conversations with his parents or with teachers during at least one mealtime, on 4 days in 1 week, so he can participate socially at meals.*

   Comment: This goal suffers from the use of jargon with the term *turns.* Putting the term in quotation marks suggests that it needs to be explained, but it would be better to simply not use a jargon term. The "turns" component is included to show that a monosyllabic response would not be considered having a conversation; the conversation has to last through two back-and-forths. This goal is written for school and home, although one criterion is that Desmond will converse with his parents or teachers.

4. *Desmond will move toward and stay with other children five separate times during free-choice times, such as centers, over 3 days, so he can participate socially during these routines.*

   Comment: Joining other children is spelled out in this goal. "Stay" is not defined, which could be problematic. But if an element of a goal is not defined, then it is assumed that adult judgment will be acceptable. To repeat earlier points, operationally defining terms such as *stay,* for instance by giving a criterion number of seconds, is technically better.

SUMMARY

Functional goals promote child and family success in current and future environments. They address the development of the child's skills in the home, classroom, and community. Functional goals reflect the priorities of the family, reflect real-life situations, are understandable, and have logical criteria. The true test of functionality is whether the question "Why is the child working on this goal?" can be answered. If the answer is not immediately apparent, the goal may not be necessary.

Discussion Questions

1. What are the drawbacks to using standardized developmental checklists to create goals?
2 Give three examples of functional verbs.
3. Give three examples of jargon terms to be avoided when writing goals.
4. What are the four learning stages that should be considered when writing goals?
5. Score an old IFSP or IEP using the Goal Functionality Scale II, then use the scale to score a document written with functional goals.
    a. How much do the scores differ?
    b. What differences are apparent between the documents?

Notes and Ideas

Chapter 7

Embedded Intervention

Key Points

- Embedded intervention is a recommended approach for addressing the individualized goals of children with disabilities in their natural environments.
- Incidental teaching is used
  - To encourage a child to continue a behavior for a longer amount of time (i.e., show more engagement)
  - To encourage a child to use more sophisticated and complex behavior (i.e., show a higher level of engagement)
  - To encourage a child to work toward his or her developmental goals
  - In naturally occurring situations (with what a child is already interested in)
  - In any interaction with a child and during any routine of the day, and it can address any type of developmental goal

WHAT IS EMBEDDED INTERVENTION?

Embedded intervention is a recommended approach for addressing children's individualized goals in their natural environments (Wolery, Anthony, Caldwell, Snyder, & Morgante, 2002). Implementing interventions in the classroom, in the context of ongoing routines, is a practical approach to intervention. Children learn new skills in the context in which they will use them; there is no need for them to transfer skills from a therapy context to a natural environment. Embedded intervention also provides children with multiple opportunities to learn skills throughout the day because they are addressed as the need for them naturally arises. Finally, embedded intervention supports classroom membership and puts the focus on children's independence and engagement.

MOLLY ASSUMED THAT HER class of preschoolers was just an energetic group. The children often flitted from one activity to another during free play, never sitting down and attending to an activity for a long period of time. When the children did choose a center to play in, Molly noticed that they often played in a simplistic way, not interacting with each other very much, not pretending, and not creating things. She had set goals for the children at the beginning of the year, but she found that she rarely pulled children aside to address the goals anymore because the children were not attentive to the individualized tasks she prepared for them. A fellow teacher suggested that the problem in Molly's room might not be overly energetic children but an environment that created low engagement levels.

INCIDENTAL TEACHING

One strategy for embedding interventions in classroom routines is incidental teaching. Incidental teaching is a method for elaborating on or expanding children's existing engagement (Hart & Risley, 1975). In other words, incidental teaching involves paying attention to what children are already interested in and helping them do more with it. It is a strategy for teaching, using naturally occurring situations (children's interests) rather than out-of-context or forced, nonpreferred activities. In addition, incidental teaching is a method for expanding children's engagement, either across time or to more sophisticated levels.

Many teachers know about "teachable moments." There are almost unlimited opportunities for teaching in early childhood, and teachers and caregivers are teaching children at all times whether they know it or not. Incidental teaching is a way of systematizing this somewhat natural teaching.

Much of what adults know has been acquired by participating in activities of interest to them. For instance, adults often learn new vocabulary by imitating those around them, gain geographic knowledge by traveling, and learn about other cultures by watching movies (Schank & Cleary, 1995). They do not sit down and intentionally try to learn or memorize these facts; instead, they acquire them through their natural interests. Incidental teaching is a strategy to help children learn through activities that they are interested in rather than through memorization. The term *incidental* means that something occurs by chance or without intention or calculation. Incidental teaching, then, is using children's natural interests to insert opportunities to use teaching techniques. In the course of doing something fun, children learn without noticing that an adult was teaching.

Incidental teaching has its roots in three traditions: behaviorism, ecological theory, and constructivism. Behaviorally, incidental teaching is the systematic application of prompts, contingent on child behavior. In other words, adults start by providing the least amount of assistance possible to encourage a child to display more engagement or more sophisticated behavior. If the child does not respond or is still not displaying the level or amount of engagement that the adult would like, the assistance provided becomes gradually more instructive. In addition to using prompts, incidental teaching also requires the use of other environmental demands that are consistent with ecological theory in early childhood special education. This theory includes the principle that instruction and other interventions (e.g., therapies) should be consistent, including environmental demands such as the activity, the location, and the other people present. To be consistent with this principle, incidental teaching always occurs in the context of ongoing routines. Finally, incidental teaching is a part of *scaffolding,* a term coined in constructivist early childhood education (Vygotsky, 1978). Incidental teaching involves eliciting elaborations of what the child is already doing and is, therefore, similar to Vygotsky's notion that learning occurs within the zone of proximal development. Incidental teaching can be considered one of the most theoretically eclectic practices in early childhood education.

A few points about incidental teaching must be made before describing its benefits and how to implement it.

1. *Adults differ in how much and how well they naturally teach children.* Some adults read children's cues better than do other adults. Some know how to scaffold better, have a better understanding of developmentally appropriate extensions of the child's current interests, or know how to make the current activity more interesting to prolong the child's engagement. People who are considered "good with children" are often successful natural teachers, but some adults need to be trained in basic adult–child interactions.

2. *Some environments provide more teachable moments than others.* Interesting spaces, situations, and activities are more conducive to incidental teaching than are lackluster ones. When children's interest is piqued, adults have clear opportunities to teach. Not everything has to be novel, however. Children often have familiar interests—materials and activities they go back to time and time again. As long as children are either fascinated (which tends to be a temporary condition) or absorbed (which is often a constant condition with respect to the current object of their engagement), teachers have prime teachable moments. They should strive, therefore, to make the environment as interesting as possible.

3. *Some children give adults more opportunities for teaching than do others.* Children who are active, zestful, and sociable almost demand adult attention, which means they are likely to be taught. In contrast, children who are passive, quiet, and withdrawn might inadvertently be overlooked by adults and receive less teaching. Some children have challenging behaviors that cause teachers to interact with them often, but with more emphasis on getting them to stop doing things than on teaching content (i.e., concepts, skills, the curriculum, or their IFSP or IEP outcomes or goals). Teachers need to ensure that *all* children receive learning opportunities.

4. *Informal, natural teaching might inadvertently teach behaviors adults did not intend.* Adult attention is usually reinforcing, meaning that it serves to increase the likelihood of recurrence of the behavior being attended to. So, when adults pay attention to children when they are doing unacceptable or undesired things, they might be teaching children to do those things more. This seems counterintuitive to many adults, because the adult attention seems aversive (e.g., the adult is scolding the child). Nevertheless, even negative statements by the adult, such as "Stop that," "Don't do that," "No," and so forth, can actually be reinforcing. It likely has something to do with children's desire to have some control over their environment. Many children engage in behavior that gives them a sense of control; this is natural and positive when channeled correctly. The reinforcement value of adult attention is also understandable considering how children react to adults: Adults have high social value (i.e., most children love most of their natural caregivers). Teachers, therefore, need to be careful about what they attend to—what they teach.

5. *Informal, natural teaching might not be successful for specific behaviors that adults want children to display.* Although good early childhood practices, including developmentally appropriate practices, can be beneficial to children with special needs, almost by definition they are unlikely to be enough to help children meet their goals (Wolery, Strain, & Bailey, 1992). Furthermore, if the incidental teaching episode is to involve systematic means of eliciting higher-level behavior, the informal approach might not include such direct attention to specific goals. Teachers, therefore, should build attention to specific goals *into* natural teaching (i.e., embed opportunities to practice specific skills into daily activities, sometimes planning for the use of specific instructional strategies) instead of adding attention to specific goals *on to* natural teaching (i.e., pulling the child aside for extra practice).

What Are the Benefits of Incidental Teaching?

Incidental teaching is useful because teaching opportunities arise from following a child's lead (rather than from imposing the teacher's plan on the child), ensuring that teaching occurs in activities the child enjoys. This can help to reduce problem behavior the child might exhibit when frustrated with task demands. In addition, incidental teaching is beneficial because it can be used to expand the child's engagement across time, across behaviors, and toward developmental goals.

Following the Child's Lead

During incidental teaching, the adult pays attention to what the child is already interested in and helps the child expand his or her engagement with the item or activity of interest. The benefits of orienting to the child's interests are that 1) the child is more likely to be engaged with the activity enough to turn it into a teaching opportunity and 2) the adult can model skills that the child is likely to use because those skills are functional in preferred activities.

Following the child's lead is important because children are more likely to persist in working toward developmental goals if teaching occurs in an activity the child prefers. For example, if a child has difficulty pronouncing the letter *L,* the teacher can model and reinforce the skill throughout the day, in context. If the teacher pulls the child out of an ongoing activity and has the child repeat a list of words that include the letter *L,* however, the child will probably get frustrated with the task because he or she will perceive it as not being nearly as interesting as what his or her peers are engaged in. If the children are building with LEGOs, the teacher could take charge of block distribution and have all children verbally request the blocks they need. Having the child request "Yellow LEGO, please" promotes pronunciation practice just as effectively as reciting a list of words and is more fun and functional for the child.

Incidental teaching also allows adults to model how the child can expand on play schemes that the child uses regularly. For example, if a child's preferred activity center is the housekeeping center (child-size plastic appliances, pretend food, dolls, and dress-up clothes), the teacher can model more sophisticated play for the child. The housekeeping center would be a suitable zone in which to encourage pretend play. The acquisition of symbolic (e.g., pretend) play is a developmental milestone. Sorting skills can be practiced with the pretend food, multiple-step tasks can be practiced by "preparing" a meal, and self-help skills (such as buttoning a shirt) can be practiced with dress-up clothes or by caring for dolls. Therefore, even though a child might continue to return to the same activity, he or she will learn to add on to it and can continue to learn from it if the teacher attends to the child's preferred activity and uses it to model skills.

One method of initiating incidental teaching interactions is to employ *joint attention strategies.* Using joint attention, either the teacher or the child indicates to the other that he or she is interested in an object or activity. For example, if a child is banging two blocks together, the teacher could get two or three more blocks and build a tower. When the teacher says, "Look!" and points to the tower, she is showing the child that she is interested in the blocks, too. Thus, both partners in the interaction are focusing on one object. This is sometimes known as *triadic communication,* with the two interaction partners and the object forming the triad. This type of interaction can be helpful for generating expansions; because the child is interested in the object (i.e., engaged), the teacher's elicitation of more sophisticated behavior with the object builds on (i.e., scaffolds upon) the child's engagement. This makes incidental teaching a responsive, strengths-based (or asset-based) approach to early education.

Expanding the Child's Engagement

Incidental teaching can also be used to encourage the child to expand his or her engagement. Engagement can be expanded in three ways: 1) more engagement, 2) higher engagement, and 3) work toward developmental goals.

More engagement refers simply to getting the child to spend a longer amount of time engaged in whatever the child is doing. For example, if a child has drawn a picture for his or her mother, the teacher might encourage the child to draw one for his or her father as well. Doubling the size of the child's project increases the amount of time that the child spends engaged in the activity. More engagement is beneficial because the longer a child is engaged with an activity, the more teaching opportunities that will be present.

Higher engagement refers to getting the child to increase the complexity and sophistication of his or her behavior in the current activity. For example, if a child who is capable of drawing pictures is mindlessly scribbling, the teacher might encourage the child to draw something recognizable. In addition, the teacher might ask the child to explain the picture when it is completed. Planning and executing the drawing of a recognizable object or scene and explaining the drawing to another person require more complex engagement than does random scribbling. Encouraging higher engagement is beneficial because children learn more when engaged at higher levels. Table 7.1 provides a summary of the levels of engagement complexity (the lowest form of engagement is found at the bottom, progressing upward to the highest form at the top).

Engagement can also be expanded by encouraging the child to work toward his or her developmental goals. Any goal can be addressed, whether it is a goal set by the parent or teacher or an outcome that is written in an IFSP or IEP. Incidental teaching allows the child's goal to be addressed in the child's daily context. For example, if a child who struggles with receptive language is playing in the housekeeping center, the teacher could take advantage of the child's in-

Table 7.1. Levels of engagement complexity

Type of engagement	Levels of complexity
Sophisticated engagement	Persistence
	Symbolic behavior (pretend play, talking about someone or something that is not present)
	Context-bound, understandable language
	Constructive behavior (making, creating, building)
Average engagement	Active interaction with the environment (excluding those listed above)
Focused attention	Intent watching or listening
Unsophisticated engagement	Repetitive, simple, low-level behavior
	Casual attention (scanning the environment)
Nonengagement	Unoccupied behavior (waiting needlessly, staring blankly, wandering aimlessly, crying, acting aggressively)

terest to work on language skills. The teacher could address comprehension skills by asking the child to bring her an orange, a green pepper, and a piece of bread on a blue plate. The teacher could help the child practice multiple-step commands by having him or her make a pancake by pouring the batter, flipping it with a spatula, and putting it on a plate. Learning language skills in context is much more interesting and useful to children than having them sit down with a stack of flashcards.

MOLLY NOTICED THAT ONE child in her class, Joey, was particularly prone to low levels of engagement during free play. Joey often stood and looked around the room while mindlessly twisting hair around his finger. When he did play with materials, it always involved rolling toy cars back and forth in the block center. Molly realized that it was easy for the classroom staff to overlook Joey's low engagement because he did not display any challenging behaviors; Molly was concerned, however, that Joey's play was not differentiated enough for learning to occur.

How Do I Use Incidental Teaching?

Incidental teaching can be used during any interaction with a child, during any routine. The key to incidental teaching is to be attentive to what children are interested in during each routine of the day and to use their interest to promote more engagement, higher engagement, or work toward developmental goals.

Incidental teaching is easiest to implement in engaging environments. Providing a variety of interesting activities and materials increases the chances that children will initiate an interaction. Teachers might also consider setting up an appealing activity and setting out all needed supplies except for one. For children to participate in the task, they will need to request the needed material or problem-solve to either obtain the material themselves or find a substitute for it. This strategy can create more engagement (children are engaged in the task longer by taking time to solve the problem), create higher engagement (children are required to request assistance or use problem-solving skills), and be used to work toward children's developmental goals (e.g., point to needed material, verbally request assistance, brainstorm alternate solutions).

MOLLY EXAMINED HER classroom environment and decided to make it more interesting for the children. She decorated the walls with colorful pictures of animals, cutouts of letters and numbers, and unusual shapes and scenes. When she was finished, the classroom looked more inviting and fun, and the children had a number of items to comment on, ask questions about, and label. Molly thought that the reason the children had been engaging in unsophisticated play was that they had already mastered the toys she had available for them, so she bought toys that required a higher skill level. She even bought some toys that she knew would be difficult for the children to operate, but she wanted to challenge them and require them to use persistence and problem-solving skills. In addition, Molly made a point of planning at least one novel activity for the children each week, such as making snow cones, planting a flower, or taking a nature hike.

Incidental teaching can be used to address any number of goals during a particular routine, but the most functional goals to be addressed with incidental teaching are those that are meaningful in that routine. For instance, social skills, such as following routines and interacting with a group, are better addressed during circle time, whereas fine motor skills, such as pincer grasp and eye–hand coordination, are better addressed during meals and art activities. Incidental teaching is easier to implement when the child has functional goals because opportunities for teaching the skill will arise more frequently if the skill is needed in the child's daily con-

Table 7.2. Points to remember about incidental teaching

Pay attention to the child's interests.
Teach in context (functional skills).
Provide an engaging environment.
Give the child no more help than is necessary.
Encourage more engagement, higher engagement, or working toward a goal.

text. It is important to remember that the child should be given no more than the minimal amount of help needed to complete the task. Skill development will be more rapid if the teacher expects the child to complete tasks independently and provides assistance only when necessary. The child should be given ample time to respond to a request before the teacher prompts the child, answers a question for him or her, or completes part of a step in the task. Table 7.2 provides a summary of points to keep in mind about incidental teaching.

Almost any skill can be addressed using incidental teaching. For example, cognitive skills (concept development and problem solving) could be addressed during circle time by reading the beginning of a story and having children brainstorm about what the character might do next or how the story might end. The key is to read enough of the story so children are interested in sticking with it and hearing how it ends. The teacher takes advantage of child interest and increases engagement from focused attention to sophisticated engagement through the questions and answers. Language skills (communication and speech) could be addressed throughout the day by asking a child to explain what he or she is drawing or building. Gross motor skills (movement and independent positioning) could be addressed during outside play by reinforcing the child's behavior (with either verbal praise or earned points), which will encourage him or her to play for a longer amount of time. Fine motor skills (handling materials and eye–hand coordination) could be addressed during snack time or lunch by giving the child a variety of utensil types and sizes and a variety of food sizes and textures to work with. Social skills (following routines and participating in interactions) could be addressed by creating situations in which peers are playing with another child's preferred item, which provides incentive for the child to join the peers. Finally, self-help skills (feeding, dressing, and toileting) could be addressed during play with dress-up clothes or by introducing and explaining skills in the context of caring for dolls in the housekeeping center.

MOLLY DECIDED TO START using incidental teaching across the routines in the children's day. When she noticed that children chose an activity during free play, she would give them extra attention by asking the children about the activity, commenting on their actions, or giving them extra materials to use in their play. She noticed that giving the children a little bit of extra attention was usually all it took to keep them engaged in the activity longer or to encourage them to use higher levels of engagement. She also realized that peer interaction was a good way to help the children stay engaged in an activity or increase the complexity of their play, so she made a point of encouraging social activities.

Molly also used incidental teaching to help Joey increase the sophistication of his engagement. When he casually looked around the room, Molly invited Joey to play. When Joey joined an activity that Molly was already involved in, she let him decide how he wanted to participate in the activity and then reinforced his choice and helped him to stay engaged. When Joey initiated play with the toy cars, Molly joined him in the block center and helped him to become engaged at a higher level of sophistication. For example, Molly would ask Joey where the cars were traveling or help him build roadways and garages. Using incidental teaching, Molly was able to increase the sophistication of Joey's play by engaging him at higher levels of complexity in his preferred task and encouraging his participation in nonpreferred tasks.

Molly also began to address the goals she had set for the children. Instead of pulling children out of activities and presenting them with an individual task that targeted their goals, she looked for teaching opportunities within the activities children were already engaged in. The children made rapid progress toward their goals because skills were being addressed in functional, interesting contexts. Molly also felt that she was able to address more goals for more children because she was embedding the individualized goals into group activities rather than trying to find time to pull the children out for special attention.

Incidental teaching produced positive effects in Molly's classroom. The children spent more time engaged in activities and less time flitting from one center to another. Their play behavior increased in sophistication. In addition, Molly was able to help each child work toward his or her goals by embedding intervention in activities that were interesting and preferred by the children.

Keep in mind that incidental teaching is often used naturally by teachers. As long as teachers are talking about or doing something children are interested in, child engagement is being promoted. Teachers can always use more incidental teaching, though. Data indicate that rates of incidental teaching in inclusive preschool classrooms are low (Casey & McWilliam, in press). In three studies associated with the Improving Engagement in Preschoolers with Disabilities project, teachers were observed to use incidental teaching with one child with disabilities at a low rate before we trained them to use more incidental teaching. (In the first study, incidental teaching was used, on average, during 4.3 of 12 intervals that were 5 minutes in length. In the second and third studies, 15-second intervals were used. On average, teachers used incidental teaching during 2.5 and 3.8 intervals of every 120, respectively.) After training, however, all teachers were able to increase their use of incidental teaching. (In the first study, teachers were able to increase their use of the strategy to their baseline rate plus six uses per hour, and teachers in the second and third studies were able to increase their use to 19.4 and 17.0 intervals in a 120-interval observation, respectively.) This shows that it is feasible for teachers to increase their use of incidental teaching if they are conscious of its use.

WHAT DO I DO IF . . . ?

How do I find time in my day to implement incidental teaching?

Incidental teaching does not require you to give one child all of your attention at the expense of other children, activities, and tasks in the classroom. Incidental teaching is merely good teaching—interaction, praise, and interest. Interactions with a child do not have to be long to be productive.

Remember that incidental teaching can be used during any interaction with a child. Use incidental teaching during routines that would be happening in your classroom anyway, and they will not take any time out of your schedule. If a child needs your assistance with hand washing, turning the routine into a teaching opportunity is more productive than washing the child's hands yourself in silence. Ask the child what the steps in the hand-washing routine are. Have him or her complete the steps with minimal assistance. While the child is washing, express curiosity about why his or her hands were blue. Was he or she painting? If so, what did the child create? Ask the child to think about what things besides paint could turn his or her hands blue.

Finally, incidental teaching does not have to be a one-on-one teaching strategy. You can encourage a group of children who are playing together to play longer by joining the activity and expressing interest in their play scheme. More sophisticated engagement (talking and pretend play) can often be encouraged by promoting peer interaction.

How do I follow a child's lead and expand on his or her interest if the child is nonengaged?

When you see that a child is nonengaged, first engage the child in an activity or interaction. The type of approach strategy you use to do this depends on the child's history of interests. Simply inviting the child to join an ongoing activity or giving the child a choice of two previously preferred options is effective for some children. With other children, you may need to physically redirect them to an activity center, model a skill, or use hand-over-hand teaching methods to initiate participation in an activity.

Once the child is involved with the environment, it is important to continue to improve the child's level of engagement to prevent nonengagement from recurring. Attend to what the child has become interested in and use that interest as the basis for incidental teaching strategies. Incidental teaching should be used to encourage the child to continue his or her engagement and to redirect the child from nonengagement.

How do I determine the child's current interest if he or she has severe disabilities? What do I try to elicit?

Watch and listen carefully. Something as simple as a gaze shift might indicate that something or someone has caught the child's attention. You might respond by naming the item or person the child is looking at, looking at the same thing yourself, or commenting on the focus of attention. Then wait for the child to respond. The response could be another gaze shift, a smile, motor activity, or eye contact with you. When the child responds, reward the response by continuing the interaction or retrieving the item the child was focusing on.

INCIDENTAL TEACHING CHECKLIST

A checklist can be used to ensure that incidental teaching is being properly implemented in the classroom. A fellow staff member (e.g., assistant teacher from the same classroom, program director, classroom consultant, other available adult) observes the teacher for 15 minutes while he or she interacts with children during a classroom activity. The observer rates the teacher on whether he or she 1) had interesting activities and materials present for the children to talk about or do; 2) planned developmentally appropriate activities; 3) rotated activities and varied materials (either within the activity or since the previous observation); 4) initiated interactions based on what the children were doing; 5) allowed the children to remain engaged in the activity of their choice; 6) elicited elaboration of the amount or level of the children's engagement; 7) gave the children no more than the amount of help needed; 8) kept the children interested in something throughout the interaction; and 9) reinforced the children with attention, verbal praise, or physical contact. (A blank form of the Incidental Teaching Checklist can be found on page 157 in Appendix B.)

SUMMARY

Incidental teaching is a strategy for attending to children's interests and helping them expand their engagement. Engagement can be expanded across time (more engagement with the activity), across behaviors (more complex or sophisticated play), and toward developmental goals. Incidental teaching is easiest to implement when the classroom is an engaging environment and the children's goals are functional. It can be used during any interaction with a child, during any routine of the day.

Discussion Questions

1. What are the three ways in which child engagement can be expanded?
2. What is a naturally occurring situation?
3. What does it mean to follow the child's lead?
4. Give four examples of sophisticated engagement.
5. How do you currently work toward the goals of the children in your classroom?
   a. Do you pull children out of ongoing activities to work on goals?
   b. Do you embed skill acquisition into daily routines?
   c. Do you set functional goals for the children in your classroom?
6. How engaging is your classroom environment?
7. Brainstorm ways in which you can use incidental teaching during each routine of your day.

Notes and Ideas

Chapter 8

Integrated Specialized Services

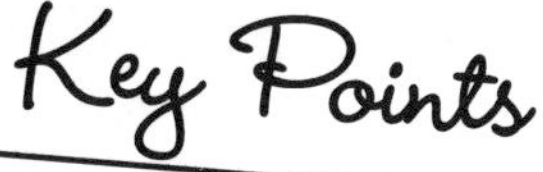

Key Points

- Using integrated specialized services, teachers and specialists can focus on skills that will be immediately useful for children.
- Using integrated specialized services, children learn skills in the contexts in which they will use them.
- Integrated specialized services allow for more practice opportunities throughout the day.
- The provision of integrated specialized services creates a stronger intervention team, because all members become more knowledgeable and skillful, and communication and collaboration increase.
- Integrated specialized services allow
  - Teachers an opportunity to observe specialists modeling specific strategies and techniques
  - Specialists an opportunity to observe teachers interact with the children
  - Specialists to see the functional contexts in which children need to perform
  - Specialists to see if interventions are being implemented in the classroom and are effective

JOCELYN, A TEACHER in a 4-year-old classroom, looked up from the block tower she was helping some children build. She saw that Alicia, the occupational therapist, had slipped in the door and was signing Benjamin out of the classroom. A moment later, Alicia asked Benjamin if he was ready to go play, took his hand, and led him out of the classroom with a brief wave to Jocelyn. Following the familiar Thursday morning routine, Jocelyn waved back and returned to her mission to help build the highest tower in the world.

WHAT ARE INTEGRATED SPECIALIZED SERVICES?

The previous vignette is probably familiar to many teachers. Children are pulled out of the classroom for therapy services and returned 30 minutes to an hour later. Teachers might not have much opportunity to talk with the specialist because he or she must get to another classroom for another child's session.

One problem with pulling children out of the classroom for therapy is that the teacher is unable to see what is occurring, ask questions, get ideas and intervention suggestions, and observe a model of appropriate intervention strategies. The amount of specific goal-directed intervention the child receives, therefore, is limited to the miniscule amount of time he or she spends with the therapists—miniscule compared to the time the child spends with the classroom staff. Expecting a child to progress with only a few minutes of intervention provided once per week—intervention that must be transferred from a therapy room to the classroom and home—is not very realistic. Imagine how much more the child would benefit if he or she were receiving intervention throughout the day, every day, because the classroom teachers knew how to address goals in daily routines. Instead of receiving only 30 or 60 minutes of specialist-provided intervention per week, the child could receive hundreds or thousands of minutes of intervention from his or her classroom teachers. This is the mission of integrated specialized services.

Integrated specialized services are therapy and special instruction provided in the classroom (or wherever other children and teachers are) in the context of ongoing routines. This method of service delivery applies to both therapists and itinerant early childhood special education teachers; collectively, these professionals will be referred to as specialists throughout this chapter. The philosophy behind integrated specialized services is that *intervention*—the child's learning opportunities—occurs between specialists' visits, during the many hours that regular caregivers, such as teachers and family members, are with the child. The small amount of time a specialist is with a child provides comparatively little intervention. Specialists provide expertise about specific methods and strategies, but it is the regular caregivers who have the opportunity to address goals every day as opportunities naturally arise. In other words, the child's regular caregivers need to own the child's goals and feel competent and responsible for addressing them rather than view goals as belonging to, and being addressed only by, the specialists.

WHAT ARE THE BENEFITS OF INTEGRATED SPECIALIZED SERVICES?

Why is it important to provide services in the classroom in the context of ongoing routines? In brief, therapy and specialized instruction are not like tennis lessons. Adults have the ability to go to a 1-hour tennis lesson and apply the skills practiced over and over in that lesson during non-lesson time, such as in a game with a real opponent. Young children, on the other hand, do not effectively learn new skills in a 1-hour therapy session; massed-trial instruction (e.g., drill work) is less effective than dispersing the trials—what we call learning opportunities—throughout the day. Children learn through exploring their environment and from their experiences, although for some children those experiences need to be manipulated to ensure that they are truly learning opportunities. Finally, young children are not easily able to transfer a newly acquired skill from one context to another. Providing services in the context in which children will use the learned skills minimizes the need for them to transfer skills from one location to another.

Integrated specialized services are not just about providing therapy in the classroom. The purposes of providing services in the classroom are for specialists to model intervention strategies for teachers, provide them with information and materials, learn from them, and learn about children's functional contexts. Therefore, one benefit of integrated specialized services is that children have multiple opportunities to practice emerging skills in multiple contexts. Teachers are aware of what children are working on and what strategies will help them achieve their goals, so they can potentially address the goals every time a need occurs in ongoing routines. Giving teachers the opportunity to see specialists model interventions benefits not only children but also teachers.

The second benefit of integrated specialized services is that caregivers are given multiple opportunities to observe interventions and learn strategies to support children's learning. The third benefit is that the specialists have multiple opportunities to share their knowledge with caregivers, receive information about children's functioning in daily routines, and observe practices that are being used in the children's natural environments. The fourth benefit is that the specialists can learn from teachers who know the children, including their interests, friends, and reactions to different approaches. The fifth benefit is that the specialists can observe the routines in which children learn, making their suggestions more relevant than they would be if children were pulled out for services.

MODELS OF SERVICE DELIVERY

Service delivery can be thought of as a continuum from segregated to inclusive methods. Table 8.1 shows six categories of service delivery: individual pull-out, small-group pull-out, one-on-one in the classroom, group activity, individualized within routines, and pure consultation (McWilliam, 1995).

Individual Pull-Out

When the specialist takes a child out of the classroom and works with him or her without regard to the classroom activities and without peer involvement, one-on-one pull-out services are being provided. Using this model, the teacher might or might not receive information from the specialist at the end of each therapy session. If so, it is usually brief and lacks demonstration.

Small-Group Pull-Out

Small-group pull-out also takes place outside of the classroom, but in this model the specialist takes the focal child and at least one other child (with or without disabilities) to a different location. Again, the teacher may or may not receive information from the specialist at the end of each therapy session.

One-on-One in the Classroom

When the specialist stays in the classroom but works with the focal child individually in a separate area of the room from the rest of the child's peers, one-on-one services are being provided in the classroom. In this model, peers are present in the classroom, but they are not intended to be involved in the therapy or specialized instruction. The teacher's role is to conduct activities with the other children in the classroom so the specialist can focus on the child being served. The teacher may or may not receive information about the session when it is over.

Table 8.1. Categories of service delivery

Model	Location	Therapy focus	Peers	Teacher's role
Individual pull-out	Anywhere apart from the regular class	Directly on child functioning	Not present	Provide information before therapy and receive information after therapy
Small-group pull-out	Anywhere apart from the regular class	Directly on functioning by child(ren) with special needs	One to six peers present	Provide and receive information before and after therapy; decide schedule with therapist and which peers will participate
One-on-one in classroom	Classroom, often apart from other children	Directly on child functioning	Present but not involved in therapy	Conduct activities, play with other children, keep children from disrupting therapy; rarely watch therapy session, provide and receive information after therapy
Group activity	Classroom; small or large group	On all children in group and on peer interactions, emphasis on meeting special needs of children	All or some children in group have special needs	When in small group, conduct activities and play with other children; if possible, watch or participate in therapist's group. When in large group, watch or participate in group activity and participate in planning large- and possibly small-group activity
Individualized within routines	Classroom, wherever focal child is	Directly but not exclusively on the focal child	Usually present	Plan and conduct activity including focal child, observe therapist's interactions with child, provide information before therapy, and exchange information with therapist after routine
Consultation	In or out of classroom	Teacher, as related to the needs of the child; can vary from expert to collegial model	Present if occurring in class; not present if occurring out of class	Exchange information and expertise with therapist, help plan future therapy sessions, give and receive feedback, and foster partnership with therapist

From McWilliam, R.A. (1995). Integration of therapy and consultative special education: A continuum in early intervention. *Infants and Young Children, 7*(4), 29–38; adapted by permission.

Group Activity

Providing services during group activities means that the specialist is in the classroom (or where other children and teachers are). The specialist usually has an agenda in mind for the therapy time, but some child-initiated activities occur. Peer involvement is high as the specialist leads an activity for a group of children. The group activity is developmentally appropriate and contains some opportunities for practice. During the group activity, the teacher is helping and watching, observing a model for how other group activities can be organized.

Individualized within Routines

An individualized-within-routines approach to service delivery means that the specialist is in the classroom (or where children and teachers are), participating in the ongoing classroom routines. Activities are developmentally appropriate and designed to enhance engagement. The level of peer involvement depends on the routine and how the child chooses to participate in it. The teacher's role is to demonstrate how the activity can be done or strategies that he or she has used to enhance engagement, and to watch the specialist to learn new strategies.

Individualized within routines is the most useful approach to service delivery because ongoing classroom routines are not disrupted and the specialist can assess children's functioning in their natural environment. In addition, the specialist has the opportunity to work within the context of children's engagement and can work with more than one child at a time. There is the potential for high peer involvement, and the teacher is able to see how interventions can fit into the regular classroom routines.

Pure Consultation

Pure consultation does not involve the child or his or her peers. In this model, the specialist and teacher evaluate the effectiveness of interventions, discuss needs, and work together to formulate solutions. The discussion can occur in the classroom or at another location. The agenda is the teacher's and specialist's, and the teacher's role is to ask for help (if needed), share information about the child's functioning, and help develop new goals and strategies.

AFTER TALKING WITH HER program director about the benefits of integrated specialized services, Jocelyn decided to try this approach. She instituted a "No Pull-Out Policy" in her classroom and told all specialists that therapy and consultation must be completed in the classroom. To make the transition to integrated specialized services easier for everyone, Jocelyn e-mailed her weekly plans to the specialists at the beginning of each week. Seeing the daily plans helped the specialists plan strategies for addressing individualized goals in the routines for which they would be present. Jocelyn also made herself available during the children's naptime on Tuesdays and after school on Thursdays to meet with any specialist who wanted to plan a group activity or consult about children or activities in the classroom.

One therapist, Alicia, approached Jocelyn and said, "I have a problem—actually a number of problems—with your new policy. First, Benjamin is too distractible to work with in the classroom. I can get a lot more out of him if I take him to the therapy room like I've been doing all year. Second, I don't think it's your place to say where therapy should be provided. I'm the one with training in this area. Third, with all due respect, you are not trained to provide therapy to children. Fourth, you seem to expect me to go beyond the treatment plan I have drawn up. Well, that violates my scope of practice, so there are ethical and maybe even legal issues involved. Fifth, my license is on the line here. If I don't provide therapy like I've been doing, I could be in violation of the licensure requirements. Sixth, I don't think I can get reimbursed for just playing around in the classroom, following the child's lead, watching you play with the kids, and so on. So, basically, I don't think this is going to work very well."

Jocelyn responded, "I'll be happy to go through each of those concerns one by one. Would that help?"

"Um, I guess so, but really I don't think I'll be able to do this."

"No, really, I'm happy to address each one of your points. Should we do it now or set up a time for later?"

"I'll talk to the supervisor of therapists," Alicia said. It was obvious that she had no interest in hearing Jocelyn's rejoinders.

"I'll be glad to talk to her, if you can give me her number," Jocelyn said.

"I don't remember it. I'll have to go by and see her."

Jocelyn watched Alicia head out to her car, already with a cell phone pressed to her ear. She didn't get a chance to tell her the following:

1. Children need to learn in distractible environments, and adults need to learn how to teach them in distractible environments. Children do not function in isolation all of the time.
2. Jocelyn wanted to collaborate with Alicia to maximize this particular child's learning opportunities. Specialists' therapeutic training often is only in clinical settings and rarely involves methods for decision making about models of service delivery such as the location of services.
3. Jocelyn did not see her role as providing therapy to Benjamin; she would be carrying out interventions to meet his IEP goals. Teachers should be able to intervene in all areas of development. Jocelyn would be carrying out Alicia's recommendations in the same way a parent would in home-based services.
4. Pediatric therapy, especially with preschoolers, is acknowledged by all professions as relevant to play, activities of daily living, and social interactions—or, as we say in our model, engagement, independence, and social relationships. Alicia was not being asked to program or provide therapy in areas outside her specialty.
5. Providing services in the classroom does not violate licensing standards in any of the professions in any state.
6. Alicia was belittling the individualized-within-routines model, but regardless, therapy delivered in any location is usually reimbursable. Payers do not usually specify the location of services. If this really became a question, Jocelyn herself could contact whoever was doing the reimbursement to find out their policy; sometimes, specialists do not cite the policy accurately, for a number of reasons.

Jocelyn did not know whether to be relieved that she did not have to go through these items with Alicia or frustrated that she did not get an opportunity to do so. Either way, it sounded as though Alicia was not going to listen. Jocelyn quickly dialed her supervisor to get administrative support, including having her call the supervisor of therapists.

THE TEACHER'S ROLE IN INTEGRATED SPECIALIZED SERVICES

When services are provided in the classroom in the context of ongoing routines, the teacher's role is to 1) observe the strategies the specialist uses, 2) consult with the specialist, and 3) show the specialist how routines work and how the child performs in the classroom.

Observation

Teachers should not be shy about watching what the specialist does with the child, asking questions, and having the specialist model or clarify the strategies being used. A specialist might work with a child for only 30 minutes per week; because the teacher is with the child daily, he or she can and should work on the child's goals when the specialist is not present. The specialist can brainstorm with the teacher about the best ways to work on the child's goals during classroom activities.

Consultation

Consultation is the exchange of information between a child's caregivers (i.e., teachers and parents) and his or her specialists (i.e., service providers). In a child care setting or preschool, consultation enables the teacher and specialist to discuss interventions, activities, child progress, and how things are going for the child in general. The three main points addressed during consultation are 1) what skills or behaviors the specialist works on with the child and how, 2) how well the strategies work, and 3) feasible strategies the teacher can use in the classroom when the specialist is not present. The consultation described here is no different from the activities involved in the pure consultation model of service delivery; however, in other models of service delivery consultation tends to occur in the classroom and be relatively brief. (A checklist for consulting with specialists can be found on page 158 in Appendix B.)

It is true that specialists have expert knowledge about their field and have ideas for new and helpful teaching strategies. Teachers, however, have expert knowledge about classroom demands, classroom opportunities, and children's functioning in classroom activities. Consultation is a two-way process, and teachers should feel free to give information to specialists in addition to receiving information from them.

Demonstration

Teachers establish the context in which children learn during the numerous hours they are in school. A vital role for them is to show specialists what goes on during classroom routines so the specialists can make relevant suggestions. Furthermore, teachers have more experience than the specialists with the child, so they know better what the child is interested in, who and what the child likes to play with, and how best to approach the child. This information can be extremely valuable for specialists. Teachers should be aware, then, that integrated specialized services are about the exchange of knowledge and skills; it is not a one-way street.

ALICIA WAS TOLD TO COOPERATE with Jocelyn, that Jocelyn's policy was consistent with recommended practice (Sandall, McLean, & Smith, 2000), that research supported her policy (McWilliam, 1996a), and that there were no studies to show that pull-out was more effective. After a couple of months, Jocelyn and Alicia were both comfortable with their new Thursday morning routine. Alicia continued to visit Benjamin at that time, but instead of pulling him out of the classroom for services she stayed in the classroom and addressed his goals during ongoing routines.

One particular morning, Alicia joined Benjamin at the table for snack time and worked with him to practice scooping cereal onto his spoon and getting it to his mouth without spilling it. Because the other children in the classroom were also eating snack, Jocelyn was able to sit at the table and be attentive to all of the children while observing the strategies Alicia was using to provide graduated guidance to Benjamin. Jocelyn took a special spoon out of the cabinet to show to Alicia. Benjamin's mother had brought it to school and asked if it would be appropriate for Benjamin, as it had a bigger, easy-to-grip handle, and Jocelyn had promised to ask Alicia's opinion on it. Alicia agreed that using the spoon was worth a try and presented it to Benjamin to see how he responded to it. She also gave Jocelyn tips for using the spoon on subsequent days.

SUMMARY

Integrated specialized services occur when therapy and specialized instruction are provided in the classroom, with other children present, in the context of ongoing routines. The teacher's role is to teach and care for children (including embedding interventions into developmentally appropriate routines between the specialist's visits); the specialist's role is to support teachers by providing information, materials, and emotional support. One way of providing such information is to demonstrate for the teaching staff. The goals for integrated specialized services are that teachers observe specialists when they are in the classroom and that teachers and specialists consult with one another.

Discussion Questions

1. What are the two hands-on integrated models of service delivery?
2. What are three advantages of integrated specialized services?
3. What are three things the teacher should do while the specialist is in the room?
4. Why do pull-out services have limited, if any, effectiveness? Give three reasons.
5. Identify three barriers that specialists might put up when asked to consider integrated services. For each barrier, provide a rejoinder.

Notes and Ideas

Planning for and Monitoring Engagement in the Classroom

Measuring Opportunities for Embedding Individual Goals

The previous chapters explain how to address children's engagement in the classroom. Planning to address engagement is only half of the battle, however; you must monitor children's engagement to ensure that your plans are having the intended effect. Section IV presents tools for measuring individual and classwide engagement, and Chapter 9 presents opportunities for embedding individual goals. The three measures discussed in this chapter will help you plan opportunities for embedding individualized intervention throughout the day, record the frequency with which individualized goals are addressed during classroom routines, and assess ecological congruence—the fit between a child and his or her environment.

Intervention Matrix

Key Points

- The Intervention Matrix (McWilliam, 1992b) is used to plan opportunities for embedding individualized intervention throughout the day.
- The Intervention Matrix provides teaching staff with a one-page summary of high-priority goals and the routines in which they should be addressed.
- The Intervention Matrix helps staff focus on specific objectives during normal classroom routines and reminds staff of family-selected priorities.

What Is the Intervention Matrix?

The Intervention Matrix (McWilliam, 1992b) is a planning tool for teachers. It requires teachers to decide during which routines they will address a child's individualized goals. It also serves as a one-page summary of the child's highest priority goals (as determined by the family) and the number of routines in which each goal should be addressed. This is particularly helpful in classrooms that have a lot of adults entering and leaving the classroom (e.g., student teachers, parent volunteers, specialists) because it enables individuals who are not familiar with a child to identify easily the skills to work on during particular activities.

Using the Intervention Matrix

The Intervention Matrix is a grid listing classroom routines across the top. An individual child's goals should be listed in the Objective column in priority order (as established by the family when the goals were written). The highest priority goal should be listed first. A checkmark should be placed in each square of the grid to indicate during which routine a particular goal could be addressed (see Figure 9.1; a blank form can be found on page 159 of Appendix B.)

Be realistic when planning opportunities for embedding intervention. Not every goal can be addressed in every routine. The highest priority goals (those listed first) should be addressed in more routines than the lower priority goals.

The grid also includes a column for indicating which adults will be responsible for addressing each goal. In classrooms in which the adults remain consistent, a specific individual could be listed. For classrooms that have a number of adults entering and leaving throughout the day, it is recommended that a general description of the adult responsible be listed (i.e., *classroom staff* as opposed to *specialist*).

TEACHER VERONICA MARTINEZ and John Simpson's parents assessed his needs for engagement, independence, and social relationships in his home and classroom routines, and his parents selected the eight goals ("objectives" on the form) shown in Figure 9.1. The goals were listed on the matrix in the priority order the parents had determined. Veronica was listed as responsible for working on every goal, and the family was also listed for the five goals that could be addressed during home routines. Beside each goal, Veronica indicated with an X the routine in which the skill was needed or where it would be a good opportunity to address the skill. She was careful not to overwhelm either the number of routines per goal or the number of goals per routine. This would keep the work manageable but still ensure that John had plenty of intervention. As can be seen in Figure 9.1, Veronica came up with 22 Goal by Routine learning opportunities per day for John. She knew, however, that he really had more learning opportunities than the form showed because within any one routine multiple opportunities for incidental teaching could occur. Veronica also knew that "Home" is an amalgamation of a number of routines, so this classroom-based matrix underestimated, in a number of ways, the total amount of learning opportunities John had throughout the day. Still, Veronica was happy that she now had a way of efficiently looking at John's goals as she planned her day to see what goals needed to be embedded in the running of each activity or routine.

WHAT DO I DO IF . . . ?

What do I do if a goal can be addressed in every routine, such as a social relationship goal?

The matrix provides guidance about optimal times to address each goal, rather than all of the times to address it.

The Intervention Matrix

Child's name: *John Simpson* ID: *1234* Begin date: *6/26/07* End date: *9/26/07*

Directions

1. List the IFSP/IEP goals in brief form in the left-hand column, according to priority order.
2. Indicate the person responsible (T = teacher; F = family; SC = service coordinator; SE = special educator; SLP = speech-language pathologist; PT = physical therapist; OT = occupational therapist).
3. Place a √ in the grid squares corresponding to the routines in which to focus on each goal. Be realistic. Generally, the higher priority goals have more routines planned than do lower priority goals.
4. In the right-hand column, enter the number of routines planned for each goal.
5. Across the bottom, enter the number of goals targeted in each routine.
6. Add either the right-hand column or the bottom row to determine the total number of teaching opportunities. Enter the total in the bottom right-hand grid.
7. Give a copy to the parents, hang one in the classroom to serve as a reminder, and file one with the IFSP/IEP.

Priority #	Person responsible		Objective	Arrival	Free play	Meals	Structured activity	Circle	Music	Art	Outdoors	Transitions	Nap	Personal hygiene	Home	Routines planned
1	T		Participate in activities without bothering other children			X	X	X	X	X						5
2	T	F	Use utensils with little spilling			X									X	2
3	T	F	Use subject-noun-verb combinations	X		X						X			X	4
4	T	F	Use objects for a long enough time to learn from them		X		X			X					X	4
5	T		Climb on playground equipment fast enough to keep up with other children								X					1
6	T	F	Occupy himself with books or quiet toys										X		X	2
7	T	F	Wash his hands by himself and remember to do so											X	X	2
8	T		Appropriately approach other children to join them		X						X					2
Goals targeted in each routine				1	2	3	2	1	1	2	2	1	1	1	5	22

Figure 9.1. The Intervention Matrix. (From McWilliam, R.A. [1992]. *Family-centered intervention planning: A routines-based approach.* Tucson, AZ: Communication Skill Builders. [available from the author])

What do I do if a goal needs to be addressed as needed, rather than during specific routines—for instance, "playing without being aggressive to other children"?

If the goal (such as aggression toward self or others) absolutely must be addressed as needed, it can be listed in each routine with *as needed* inserted in the cells.

What do I do if I have many matrices for many children?

This is a good problem! It shows that there are goals for many children, organized by routines. This is one reason to ensure that the goals are listed in the family's order of priority. If teachers have many IFSPs or IEPs to keep up with, they will need some guidance about which goals are most important. For example, if three matrices indicate that goals can be addressed during art, and for one of the children the most important goal is to be addressed during art, then the teacher would want to ensure that this happened. If the other two plans had lower priority goals to be addressed during art, teachers might not always address them during art. Two caveats are worth mentioning: 1) Most goals can be addressed during more than one routine, so failing to address a goal during a particular routine is not catastrophic; and 2) children have multiple goals that can be addressed during any single routine, so in the previous example teachers might actually have more than three goals to address during a specific routine.

What do I do if some goals get dropped and others get added?

The priority order for all active goals should be determined, so any addition to the plan should be accompanied by an invitation to the family to change the priority order. At least, the priority of the new goal(s), relative to the remaining goals, needs to be determined.

Examination of the Implementation of Embedded Intervention, Through Observation

Key Points

- The Examination of the Implementation of Embedded Intervention, through Observation (EIEIO; McWilliam & Scott, 2001) is used to record the frequency with which individualized goals are addressed during classroom routines.
- If goals are being addressed frequently, teachers are using embedded intervention to address goals.
- If goals cannot be addressed during routines, the goals may not be functional.
- If goals can be addressed during routines but are not, teachers may need to put more effort into planning for and implementing embedded intervention.

What Is the EIEIO?

The EIEIO (McWilliam & Scott, 2001) is a document for recording the frequency with which individualized goals are addressed during classroom routines. For individual child goals, data are collected on whether the goal 1) could have been addressed during each classroom routine, 2) was addressed, and 3) was addressed appropriately. As the title of the scale implies, this tool is useful for determining whether embedded intervention is occurring in the classroom.

Using the EIEIO

To complete the EIEIO form (a blank form can be found on pages 160–161 in Appendix B), list a child's individualized goals in the far left column. Across the top of the form, list the routines during which the child will be observed. The EIEIO can be completed either during a 2-hour continuous observation (during which eight 15-minute routines are observed) or across eight routines scattered throughout the day (if specific routines are to be targeted). The person completing the EIEIO should be responsible for observing and nothing else; in other words, teachers should not be in charge of completing the EIEIO unless co-teachers are in charge of all classroom activities for the duration of the observation.

During each routine, the observer should watch all interactions with the target child. At the end of the routine, the observer indicates whether each goal could have been addressed during the routine by placing a *Y* (yes, the goal could have been addressed) or *N* (no, the goal could not have been addressed) in the column labeled *C* (could have been addressed). For those goals that could have been addressed (a *Y* is marked in the column labeled *C*), the observer indicates whether the goal was addressed. A *Y* (yes, the goal was addressed) or *N* (no, the goal was not addressed) should be placed in the column labeled *W* (was addressed). Finally, for those goals that were addressed (a *Y* is marked in the column labeled *W*), the observer indicates whether they were addressed appropriately. A *Y* should be placed in the column labeled *A* (appropriateness) if the goal was addressed appropriately, and an *N* should be placed in the column if the goal was addressed inappropriately. When determining whether a goal was addressed appropriately, the observer should consider developmental and contextual appropriateness. There is a column for recording additional notes about each routine and goal, if needed.

At the end of the observation, the observer and teachers should inspect the EIEIO document to assess the implementation of embedded intervention. If goals are being addressed frequently and appropriately, the teachers are implementing embedded intervention in order to address a child's individualized goals. If goals are not being addressed frequently, further analysis should be done. If the data reveal that goals could not be addressed during routines, this implies that goals may not be functional. The child's IFSP or IEP should be reviewed to ensure that it consists of functional goals that address engagement, independence, and social relationships. If the data reveal that goals could have been addressed during routines but were not, this implies that the teaching staff is not taking advantage of opportunities within routines to embed intervention that relates to the child's individualized goals. The teaching staff should make a point of planning the routines in which the child's goals will be addressed (the Intervention Matrix could be used) and can consult with specialists for intervention strategies, if needed.

WHAT DO I DO IF . . . ?

What do I do if teachers address the goal but use a strategy different from one demonstrated by a specialist?

More than one strategy may be appropriate. If the teacher's behavior was developmentally and individually appropriate, it counts as having been addressed (W) appropriately (A).

What do I do if I had determined a goal could not be addressed during a routine, but teachers found a way to address it anyway (W)?

If teachers found a way, your original scoring of the feasibility of addressing the goal (N) was wrong and should be changed to reflect that embedding was possible. Then, it is especially important to determine whether it was addressed appropriately (A).

What do I do if I want strategies to be listed, rather than the goals?

Strategies may be listed, but make sure everyone remembers the purpose for using the strategies. That purpose should be a functional, family-chosen goal.

Vanderbilt Ecological Congruence of Teaching Opportunities in Routines, Classroom Version

Key Points

- The Vanderbilt Ecological Congruence of Teaching Opportunities in Routines (VECTOR), Classroom Version (Casey, Freund, & McWilliam, 2004) can be used to assess ecological congruence—the fit between a child and his or her classroom environment.
- Ecological congruence is assessed by focusing on child engagement, independence, and peer interactions.
- Assessment of ecological congruence includes evaluation of both 1) the opportunities available in the environment and 2) the frequency with which the child takes advantage of the opportunities.

What Is the VECTOR?

The VECTOR (Casey, Freund, & McWilliam, 2004) is a scale for assessing the ecological congruence between a child and his or her classroom environment. *Ecological congruence* has been described by Ken Thurman (1997) and Mark Wolery and colleagues (Wolery, Brashers, & Neitzel, 2002). Wolery et al. developed an "ecological congruence assessment process" (p. 131) to address the problems of nonfunctional goals and contextually irrelevant recommendations by specialists, such as special educators and therapists. The three phases of their process were the teacher's collecting information about the child's functioning in classroom routines, summarizing that information, and discussing the information with the team.

We define *ecological congruence* as the fit between the provision of particular types of supports and the need for those supports. We developed the VECTOR as a tool to collect the necessary information to address the issues Wolery et al. (2002) described. Using the VECTOR, both the opportunities available in the environment and the frequency with which the child takes advantage of the opportunities are considered in assessing ecological congruence. Incongruence is found when the opportunities provided by the physical environment or adults in the classroom do not fit with the child's use of supports, too few opportunities are provided, or the child is not taking advantage of the opportunities provided. The VECTOR is designed to focus assessment of ecological congruence on three domains: engagement, independence, and peer interactions.

Using the VECTOR

The VECTOR was designed to be used in a classroom for children between 18 months and 5 years of age. It can be completed periodically to monitor the fit between a particular child and his or her environment, to monitor child progress, or when particular concerns have been identified about child functioning in the classroom. (A blank form can be found on pages 162–164 of Appendix B.)

To complete the VECTOR, the child should be observed for at least 10 minutes during each classroom routine. For each routine, nine items concerning the environment, adult interventions, and child performance should be rated. For the environment and adult intervention items, the frequency with which each routine provides the opportunities referred to should be rated with the scale of 1 (*rarely*) to 5 (*most of the time*). For the child performance items, the observer should indicate if the child takes advantage of the opportunities provided, using the same rating scale. Scores are entered in the white boxes on the grid.

To score the VECTOR, sum the scores given for the opportunity column (marked with an *O*) for a single routine and divide by 6; this score should be entered at the bottom of the column and the procedure repeated for each routine. Next, sum the scores for the advantage column (marked with an *A*) for a single routine and divide by 3; this score should be entered at the bottom of the column and the procedure repeated for each routine. After the analysis for each routine is done, scores can be calculated for the entire day for engagement, independence, and peer interactions. Sum the scores for opportunity (both environment and adult intervention) for all routines in the day (for engagement, independence, and peer interactions, separately), and divide by the number of routines observed; enter the score in the far right column. Next, sum the scores for advantage for all routines in the day (for engagement, independence, and peer interactions, separately) and divide by the number of routines observed; enter the score in the far right column.

The scores can be interpreted in four ways. First, to determine the overall goodness of fit between the child and his or her environment across all routines of the day, compare the opportunity and advantage scores for each routine (found at the bottom of the table). If the scores are consistently high and similar, the fit is most likely good. If the opportunity and advantage scores are all low or dissimilar, the fit between the child and his or her environment may not be good, and further analysis is needed (as explained next). To determine the fit between the environment and child for specific routines, compare the opportunity and advantage scores for each routine again (found at the bottom of the table), but refer to the data within each routine to determine why scores are incongruent. For example, if the opportunity and advantage scores for a routine are both low, look at the routine-specific data to determine where change may be needed (i.e., in the physical environment, in adult interventions, or in both). You can also examine the scores for the three areas of functioning (engagement, independence, and peer interactions) to determine where specific change may be needed.

The third way to analyze the data is to determine whether the child is taking advantage of the opportunities provided by the physical environment and adults. To do this, compare the opportunity and advantage scores for each routine at the bottom of the table. If advantage scores are low while opportunity scores are high, this suggests that the child is not taking full advantage of the opportunities provided. The teacher must determine whether this discrepancy reflects a skill deficit (the child cannot do what is offered) or a performance deficit (the child will not do what is offered).

Finally, the VECTOR scores can be used to determine and monitor the child's engagement, independence, and peer interactions across all routines of the day by examining the total child scores (far right column). If scores are lower than desired, examine individual scores across routines to determine the child's strength areas, needs, and any trends in the data.

SUMMARY

The Intervention Matrix organizes intervention plans. It demonstrates how many contexts there are for intervention; each context (i.e., routine) provides numerous learning opportunities. It actually underestimates the number of contexts because there is nothing to prevent adults from addressing goals in routines not specified on the matrix. It helps adults see, in each routine, what needs to be addressed. Finally, it shows goals in order of priority. It is a "refrigerator door tool," meaning that it is on one sheet of paper and is meaningful and therefore likely to be found on a family's refrigerator door.

The EIEIO is used to record the frequency with which individualized goals are addressed in classroom routines. For each goal, during each routine, an observer rates whether the goal could have been addressed, was addressed, and was addressed appropriately. The tool helps teachers determine if they are using embedded intervention to address goals.

The VECTOR can be used to assess the ecological congruence between a child and his or her classroom environment. For each routine, an observer rates the child across three domains (engagement, independence, and peer interactions) on the number of opportunities provided by the physical environment and adult interventions and the frequency with which the child takes advantage of these opportunities. Incongruence between a child and his or her environment can be resolved by making changes to the environment, adjusting the expectations for the child or activity, or intervening with the child to teach a particular skill.

Discussion Questions

1. How are goals ordered on the Intervention Matrix?
2. When is the Intervention Matrix developed?
3. Who should have copies of the Intervention Matrix?
4. Should the Intervention Matrix be posted on walls?
5. What does the EIEIO measure?
6. How long should one observe a routine to score the EIEIO?
7. For whom would scoring the EIEIO be useful?
8. How often should a teacher and child be observed in a routine to obtain reliable information?
9. What is the purpose of the VECTOR?
10. What two things should be assessed to determine ecological congruence?
11. How do you determine the overall goodness of fit between a child and his or her environment?

Notes and Ideas

Measuring Classwide Engagement with the Engagement Check II

Key Points

- The Engagement Check II (McWilliam, 1999) is a method for determining the percentage of children engaged in classroom activities.
- The length of time between engagement checks can be adjusted to meet the needs of a particular classroom or program.
- The Engagement Check II helps teachers become more aware of group engagement during routines and can help them determine which routines tend to result in low and high engagement.

WHAT IS THE ENGAGEMENT CHECK II, AND WHY IS IT BENEFICIAL?

The Engagement Check II (McWilliam, 1999) is a method for recording group engagement; in other words, the measure allows teachers to determine the percentage of children engaged in an activity at any given time. The measure is a modification of the Planned Activity Check (Risley & Cataldo, 1973). The Engagement Check II can be used to determine the percentage of children engaged in a particular routine or to determine the percentage of children engaged across the entire day (Ridley & McWilliam, 2001). The Engagement Check II is beneficial because it is a feasible data collection tool that not only provides information about children's engagement but also guides teacher planning.

Feasibility

Collecting data with the Engagement Check II is feasible because of the tool's versatility. As will be explained next, the intervals between data collection can be adjusted to fit the needs of a particular program or classroom. The tool can also be used to assess group engagement in a specific routine, for a specific amount of time, or for the entire day. Only two numbers need to be recorded on the form for each interval; additional calculations are done after the observation.

Guiding Teacher Planning

If the Engagement Check II is used to assess group engagement during specific routines, teachers will have data about the percentage of children they are able to engage in the activity. If a routine frequently yields a low percentage of group engagement, teachers might be wise to change the routine to make it more appealing for the children. On the other hand, if group engagement is frequently high in a specific routine, teachers will know that a particular child who struggles with engagement might need to be taught how to participate in the activity. The Engagement Check II is also useful for tracking group engagement across time. Teachers may decide to alternate toys or switch activity themes when they realize that group engagement is beginning to decrease.

EDITH, THE EDUCATIONAL coordinator for an inclusive preschool program, was proud to report that the program had received the highest marks on the latest state assessment. Although Edith was extremely pleased with the results, she also realized that the assessors had mostly looked at the physical environment and health and safety precautions. She was curious about what children were actually doing in the program, so she decided to observe each classroom and complete the Engagement Check II.

USING THE ENGAGEMENT CHECK II

The Engagement Check II is simple to complete by conducting visual scans of the classroom. It can be completed by a classroom teacher or other observer. During each interval, the observer scans the classroom once to count how many children are present. The observer then scans the classroom a second time to count how many children are nonengaged. (The number of nonengaged children is counted and recorded because it is usually a smaller number than the amount of engaged children. Also, nonengagement is easier to spot because it is one class of behaviors; for this measure, an engaged child can display any behavior besides nonengagement.) These two numbers are the only ones recorded on the Engagement Check II Data Collection form during the observation for each interval. (A blank data collection form can be found on pages 165–166 of Appendix B.)

After the observation, the observer calculates the number of children engaged during each interval by subtracting the number of nonengaged children from the total number of children present. The number of children engaged should be recorded on the data collection form. Next, the observer calculates the percentage of children engaged during each interval by dividing the number of children engaged by the total number of children present and multiplying by 100. Finally, the average percentage of children engaged during the observation is calculated by adding the percentages of children engaged during each interval and dividing by the total number of intervals.

The interval length is flexible but should be no more than 5 minutes long. For precise measurement, it is suggested that 15-second intervals be used for a maximum of 15 minutes (60 intervals). If feasible, more than one 15-minute observation can be made in one day. For less precise measurement, the intervals can be increased to any duration up to 5 minutes. But for stable information, no fewer than 30 data points (i.e., intervals) should be amassed. For supervision purposes, intervals should be no more than 5 minutes apart. For 5-minute intervals, it is often helpful to let classroom routines determine the length of the observation (either observe all morning routines, all child-directed routines, or only one routine).

While observing the classroom, it is recommended that the observer take note of the nonengagement seen. It might be the case that a specific child is continuously nonengaged (instead of a different child being nonengaged at each interval). If this is the case, the teachers might need to teach the child how to initiate and sustain play or be conscientious of the use of incidental teaching with the child. Taking notes during the Engagement Check II observation might instead reveal that children tend to be engaged throughout the day except for high levels of nonengagement at circle time. In this case, the teachers should consider modifying the routine instead of intervening with specific children.

OVER THE NEXT 2 WEEKS, Edith observed each of the six classrooms in the program. She made a point of staying in each room for at least 2 hours in the morning so she could observe free play times, snack times, and circle times. After her observations, Edith calculated the average percentage of children engaged in each classroom. The results indicated that the average percentage of children engaged in each room was 87, 92, 90, 82, 79, and 88. Edith met with the teachers, and they set a goal that in 2 months every classroom would have an average of at least 85% of children engaged.

Sabrina, the lead teacher in the classroom who had 79% of children engaged, decided to use the Engagement Check II herself to monitor changes she was going to make in the classroom. First, she completed the Engagement Check II for an entire morning, making note of the timing of transitions between routines. She also noted when one particular child, Micah, was nonengaged because she knew he wandered aimlessly much more frequently than she would like. As can be seen in Figure 10.1, Micah seemed to be persistently nonengaged during free choice times (free play, outside, and centers), and the class in general had lower engagement levels during circle time.

Sabrina decided to reassess her circle time plans and create more interesting and interactive activities for the routine. She also decided that she and her assistant teachers should focus on teaching Micah how to choose an activity, start playing, and keep playing during free choice activities.

As Sabrina started trying new activities in circle time and started modeling appropriate play during free choice times for Micah, she completed the Engagement Check II during those specific routines to see if engagement levels were improving. By taking note of circle time activities and child engagement over a number of days, Sabrina was able to determine that interactive circle time activities, such as having children find the ingredients listed in a book and add them to the middle of the circle as the character in the book baked a cake, resulted in higher engagement than circle times that included drill work with flashcards. Sabrina and the assistant teachers also worked with Micah during free play, outside time, and centers to help him initiate and sustain play. They felt that Micah was doing a better job choosing and participating in activities, and the Engagement Check II results supported their observations—engagement levels improved during free choice activities, and Micah was not persistently nonengaged.

Engagement Check II Data Collection

Interval	Number present	Number nonengaged	Number engaged	Percentage engaged	Notes
1	6	2	4	67	ARRIVAL
2	8	2	6	75	FREE PLAY
3	12	2	10	83	
4	12	1	11	92	Micah
5	12	2	10	83	Micah
6	11	2	9	82	Micah
7	12	1	11	92	CIRCLE
8	12	2	10	83	
9	12	3	9	75	
10	12	5	7	58	SNACK
11	11	2	9	82	
12	12	1	11	92	
13	12	1	11	92	OUTSIDE
14	10	2	8	80	
15	10	1	9	90	Micah
16	12	1	11	92	Micah
17	12	2	10	83	Micah
18	12	2	10	83	
19	11	1	10	91	CENTERS
20	12	2	10	83	Micah
21	12	2	10	83	
22	11	2	9	82	Micah
23	12	2	10	83	Micah
24	12	1	11	92	
		Average percentage engaged		83	

Figure 10.1. Sabrina's Engagement Check II form.

After 2 months, Edith observed the classrooms again to see if engagement levels had improved. Indeed, Edith found that every class achieved the goal to have at least 85% of children engaged in activities. She continues to use the Engagement Check II to sporadically monitor engagement in the classrooms and encourages teachers to use it as well.

WHAT DO I DO IF . . . ?

What do I do if I want a very precise measurement of the class's engagement?

The shorter the intervals between scans, the more precise the measurement. Furthermore, the more frequently the data are collected, the more specific the information is. Therefore, to obtain precise measurement, scan the room every 15 seconds for 15 minutes and observe for 15 minutes numerous times during the day and during the week.

? What do I do if I want to know about engagement in a specific routine?

The more data obtained from a single routine, the more reliable those data are. So, if the teacher wants information about circle time, he or she should make observations during numerous circle times. We recommend at least four such observations, averaged. That is, all of the percentages of children engaged at each scan are averaged for each observation session. Then, those total scores for each day are averaged to produce a single mean percentage.

? What do I do if I want to know the general engagement level across routines?

Engagement varies by routine, so a reliable score would need to encompass numerous routines over numerous days. We recommend observing during 6 routines over 4 days and averaging all those scores.

? What do I do if I just want to get a rough estimate of engagement, without all of this frequent scanning?

It is possible to use the scanning technique of the Engagement Check II to get a rough estimate. For example, when we are observing in classrooms for consultation purposes, we make narrative notes, organized in 5-minute increments. Every 5 minutes, we scan the room once to obtain the percentage of children engaged. Although these data are not stable in a psychometric sense, they provide helpful information when added to the field notes.

SUMMARY

The Engagement Check II is the closest link to the original engagement research involving children. Knowing the percentage of children engaged during a routine or in a classroom provides a basic index of the quality of the classroom (McWilliam, Trivette, & Dunst, 1985). Unlike measures of quality that focus on environmental features, this one focuses on what children are doing (de Kruif & McWilliam, 1999). Perhaps its greatest virtue is that it can influence the priorities of the adults working in the classroom. Once teachers have been immersed in the importance of having all children be engaged, being in a classroom without frequently scanning is difficult for them. It becomes automatic and almost unconscious. Teachers who reach that level are highly likely to have an interesting classroom with myriad learning opportunities for children. A good place to start is to measure engagement with the Engagement Check II.

Discussion Questions

1. What are some advantages of measuring the percentage of children engaged?
2. Who might be good observers to use the Engagement Check II? What would they do with the data?
3. How many times should you observe a routine in 15-second intervals to get dependable scores?
4. For how long should you observe, scoring every 15 seconds?
5. How can the Engagement Check II affect a teacher's view of the purpose of early childhood education?

Notes and Ideas

Chapter 11

Measuring Individual Engagement

Whereas the previous chapter discussed the measurement of the percentage of children engaged in the classroom, this chapter discusses the measurement of the engagement of an individual child. In our research, we use precise measurement techniques, involving handheld computers and measurement of the types and forms of engagement in 15-second intervals (McWilliam & Casey, 2004); however, we have also developed rating scales that can be completed by teachers or parents. This chapter discusses each of these rating scales.

Scale for Teachers' Assessment of Routines Engagement

Key Points

- The Scale for Teachers' Assessment of Routines Engagement (STARE; McWilliam, 2000) is a tool for collecting data on an individual child's engagement.
- The STARE helps teachers determine with whom or what the child is engaged and how complex the engagement is.
- The STARE helps teachers become more aware of child engagement across all routines of the day.
- The STARE can help teachers determine which routines tend to result in low and high engagement in children.

MARK IS THE LEAD TEACHER in a preschool classroom. He is concerned about Tabitha, a child in the class who he thinks spends a great deal of time using unsophisticated behavior or staring blankly. Tabitha does not engage in the behaviors enough that they have become a big concern or attracted much teacher and parental attention, so Mark is not sure whether his suspicions about Tabitha are accurate. Mark would like to have some proof that Tabitha is having difficulty staying engaged at high levels before he attempts to design any kind of intervention for her.

WHAT IS THE SCALE FOR TEACHERS' ASSESSMENT OF ROUTINES ENGAGEMENT AND WHY IS IT BENEFICIAL?

The STARE (McWilliam, 2000) is a data collection tool designed for use by preschool teachers. Teachers observe an individual child's engagement across all routines of the day; for each routine they rate who or what the child was engaged with and how complex the child's engagement was. The purpose of the STARE is to make teachers more aware of child engagement across all routines of the day. In addition, the STARE can help teachers determine which routines, if any, are particularly difficult for a child (meaning the child tends to spend a lot of time nonengaged during the routine).

The STARE is beneficial because it is a feasible data collection tool that can be used by teachers in the course of daily activities. It provides useful information about engagement levels in individual children. In addition, it helps teachers become aware of routines that tend to result in low engagement levels in children.

Feasibility

The STARE has been used by preschool teachers as part of an ongoing research project and has proven to be a feasible data collection tool. Teachers observe the child for a limited portion of time in each routine (about 10 minutes; in general, teachers just need to be aware of the child's activity during the course of the routine) and record data by circling four ratings. Teachers can decide how often to complete the scale; in fact, completing the scale only 1 or 2 days per month produces enough data to get a reliable picture of a child's typical engagement.

Data on Individual Children

Unlike the Engagement Check II (McWilliam, 1999), which can be used to collect data about classwide engagement, the STARE is meant to be used for data collection on individual children. If a child in the classroom has difficulty with engagement, the STARE can be used to determine how he or she spends time in each activity. The STARE will help the teacher determine whom or what the child spends the majority of his or her time interacting with (adults, peers, or materials). In addition, the STARE helps the teacher determine the complexity of the child's engagement (how sophisticated the child's behavior is).

The STARE is useful for tracking a child's overall engagement across time. It can also be used to track a child's engagement in specific routines across time, making it a practical tool for measuring a child's progress in engaging in classroom routines. The STARE can help teachers determine which routines are particularly difficult for an individual child. If a teacher sees that a child is consistently rated as nonengaged during certain activities, he or she should consider modifying the routine to promote higher engagement.

Portions of this chapter are based on Casey, A.M., & McWilliam, R.A. (in press). The STARE: The Scale for Teachers' Assessment of Routines Engagement. *Young Exceptional Children.*

USING THE SCALE FOR TEACHERS' ASSESSMENT OF ROUTINES ENGAGEMENT

The STARE requires the teacher to observe a child for about 10 minutes during each routine, but this can be done *while* the teacher is teaching. In other words, the teacher simply needs to be aware of the child's activity during the routine, enough to feel like he or she has a fairly good idea of the child's behavior. The teacher should rate the child's engagement after *each routine* rather than wait until the end of the day and attempt to remember the child's behavior. The teacher will rate with whom or what the child spent the majority of his or her time and the complexity of the child's engagement. (A blank form of the STARE can be found on pages 167–169 in Appendix B.)

After observing the child in a routine, the teacher rates the amount of time the child was engaged with adults, peers, and materials. Choices range from *almost none of the time* to *half of the time* to *almost all of the time*. A separate rating should be given for adults, peers, and materials. A child may receive a high rating in more than one category. For example, if the child spends the majority of center time playing with a dollhouse with a peer (they work together to arrange furniture in the rooms and then have the play figures cook dinner together), he or she would be rated as spending *almost all of the time* with both peers and materials and perhaps *almost none of the time* with adults. Note that what is being rated is the amount of time that the child is *engaged* with adults, peers, and materials. If the child plays alongside a peer at the dollhouse but does not interact with the peer, the child would be rated as spending *almost none of the time* with peers.

The second feature of the child's engagement that should be rated is its complexity during the routine. This is a separate rating from the first one; ratings given for amount of time spent with adults, peers, and materials do not factor into ratings given for complexity of the child's engagement. There are five choices for rating the complexity of engagement. *Nonengaged* would be rated if the child engages in inappropriate behavior (aggression, breaking rules), stares blankly, wanders around aimlessly, or cries. The *unsophisticated* rating is used when the child engages in repetitive play (banging a block over and over) or casually looks around the environment without focusing on one person or thing. *Average* is rated if the child participates in the routine as expected, actively interacts with his or her surroundings, or engages in typical play. The *advanced* rating is used when the child creates, makes, or builds something or uses understandable, context-bound language (language that refers to a person or situation that is present). The *sophisticated* rating is used when a child pretends, persists at a challenging activity, or talks about someone or something that is not present.

Complexity refers to how the child spends the *most amount of time* engaged during the routine, not to the highest level of engagement that was observed. For instance, if a child spends the majority of free play looking through books but says a couple of things to a peer, rate the complexity of the child's engagement as *average* instead of *advanced*. The child spent the majority of his or her time actively interacting with materials, not talking with the peer, so *average* is the correct rating.

The STARE includes sections for a variety of routines, including arrival, circle time, centers/free play, teacher-directed activity, snack/lunch, and outside play. The STARE form also has three blank grids at the end for teachers to add additional or alternate routines.

To obtain an overall view of the child's engagement, teachers should complete the STARE about once each month. It is recommended that at least six routines be rated in the course of a single day. To track a child's engagement in a particular routine, teachers should complete the STARE more often during the specified activity only (e.g., once per week during circle time). Table 11.1 gives a summary of things to remember when using the STARE.

Table 11.1. Things to remember about the STARE

Adults refers to the regular classroom teachers, in addition to specialists, parents, volunteers, and so forth.
Materials include toys, art supplies, food, jungle gyms, and the environment in general.
Complexity refers to how the child spends the most amount of time, not to the highest level of engagement observed.
A child may receive a high rating in more than one category.
Ratings for the amount of time a child spends with adults, peers, and materials do not affect the rating for the complexity of the child's engagement.

MARK COMPLETED THE STARE for Tabitha once a week. He rated her during every routine in the day because he wanted a complete picture of her engagement. After 3 weeks, Mark looked at the data he had collected and realized that there were patterns in Tabitha's STARE ratings (see Figure 11.1). She tended to have complexity ratings of nonengaged or unsophisticated during free play and outdoor play but had higher complexity ratings during activities such as circle time and teacher-directed activities.

Mark decided that Tabitha's engagement difficulties during routines that were less structured might be due to less teacher attention. He and the assistant teacher made a point of interacting with Tabitha during less structured activities, either helping her get engaged in a task or helping her interact with peers.

After a couple of months, Mark completed the STARE for Tabitha again to see if her engagement in less structured activities had improved after the teacher intervention. He completed the STARE for another 3 weeks and found that Tabitha's engagement during less structured routines had indeed increased during the past months. He decided to complete the STARE for Tabitha at regular intervals to make sure that higher levels of engagement during specific routines were being maintained.

WHAT DO I DO IF . . . ?

How am I expected to observe a child for 10 minutes while leading circle time?

Observations of the child are to be made *while* teaching, not instead of teaching. You are not expected to observe the child for 10 uninterrupted minutes; instead, lead circle time and be aware of group engagement. The best strategy is usually to look out for atypical behavior. If you do not notice the child being particularly talkative or particularly nonengaged, you are probably safe rating him or her as having *average* engagement.

Do the best you can. One rating on one activity should never be used to make sweeping judgments about a child's engagement, so you should not be overly concerned if you have difficulties during a day's observation.

How do you rate a child during outside play?

Jungle gyms, slides, bikes, balls, and other outdoor equipment are considered to be materials. In addition, the environment in general is considered to be a material. Therefore, if a child runs around for the majority of outside play chasing his or her peers, you would rate him or her as spending *almost all of the time* with peers and materials and perhaps *almost none of the time* with adults. The complexity of the child's engagement would probably be rated as *average*.

How do you rate snack time and lunchtime?

Plates, napkins, utensils, and food are materials. Chewing is considered to be *average* engagement. Therefore, a child who sits quietly and eats his or her lunch during the designated time would be rated as spending *almost all of the time* with materials, perhaps *little of the time* with adults (some adult assistance may have been needed to open containers or cut food), and *almost none of the time* with peers (although the child sat with peers, he or she did not interact with them). The complexity of the child's engagement would be rated as *average*.

Scale for Teachers' Assessment of Routines Engagement (STARE)

Directions: Observe the child for 10 minutes in each of the following routines. First, rate the amount of time the child is engaged with adults, peers, and materials. Second, rate the complexity of the child's engagement. There is space to add additional or alternate routines at the end of the scale.

Circle time	Almost none of the time	Little of the time	Half of the time	Much of the time	Almost all of the time
With Adults	1	2	3	④	5
With Peers	1	2	③	4	5
With Materials	1	2	③	4	5
Complexity	Nonengaged 1	Unsophisticated 2	Average 3	Advanced ④	Sophisticated 5

Centers/free play	Almost none of the time	Little of the time	Half of the time	Much of the time	Almost all of the time
With Adults	①	2	3	4	5
With Peers	①	2	3	4	5
With Materials	1	②	3	4	5
Complexity	Nonengaged ①	Unsophisticated 2	Average 3	Advanced 4	Sophisticated 5

Figure 11.1. Tabitha's STARE form.

Children's Engagement Questionnaire

Key Points

- The Children's Engagement Questionnaire (CEQ; McWilliam, 1991) is a rating scale for determining the extent of a child's global engagement.
- The CEQ has been used to characterize a child's propensity for engagement, in that the rater assesses typical child behavior.
- Overall global engagement as measured by the CEQ has been found to be negatively associated with the severity of the child's functioning; that is, the more severe the child's impairments, the lower his or her global engagement ($r = -.50$, $N = 69$; McWilliam, 2005b).
- CEQ scores have not been found to be correlated with family empowerment (McWilliam, 2005b).
- The underlying structure of the CEQ comprises Competent Engagement and Unsophisticated Engagement (Snyder & McWilliam, 2006).

WHAT IS THE PURPOSE OF THE CHILDREN'S ENGAGEMENT QUESTIONNAIRE?

The purpose of the CEQ (McWilliam, 1991) is to describe a child's propensity for engagement. It is based on ratings by a person who knows the child well, such as a parent or a teacher. The 4-point rating system consists of *not at all typical, somewhat typical, typical,* and *very typical*. It can be used to describe a child's general functioning and to assess the effectiveness of the early intervention program. Unlike standardized tests, which tend to require performance with potentially unfamiliar materials in potentially unfamiliar situations, the CEQ is used to rate behavior in all situations known to the rater. Therefore, it is not a measure of developmental status. It can be used for assessing children's progress in that Competent Engagement, one of the subscales, should increase as children get older. It is not, however, an age-normed instrument, so it is best used as a way of characterizing a child, as one might do with temperament or self-regulation scales. The end of the questionnaire contains instructions for scoring the two components found in the CEQ (Snyder & McWilliam, 2006): Competent Engagement and Unsophisticated Engagement.

USING THE CHILDREN'S ENGAGEMENT QUESTIONNAIRE

The CEQ has been used in research in the United States (McWilliam, 2005b), Portugal (Aguiar, 2005), and Sweden (Almqvist, 2006). It is given to parents or other adults who know the child well. On the basis of the rater's experience with the child, the 32 behaviors are rated in terms of how typical they are for that child. Two means are computed: one for Competent Engagement and one for Unsophisticated Engagement. As is stated in the scoring section of the instrument, "Unsophisticated engagement might be expected of younger children—those who do not spend as much time engaged in purposeful play with adults, peers, and materials. Intervention should be aimed at increasing the mean rating for competent engagement." (A blank form of the CEQ can be found on pages 170–173 of Appendix B.)

SUMMARY

The STARE is a tool for collecting data on individual children's engagement. Teachers rate both the amount of time children spend engaged with adults, peers, and materials and the complexity of the child's engagement. The scale is useful for tracking a child's overall engagement or for tracking engagement in a specific routine. Use of the STARE is feasible for preschool teachers because observations of the child are short, only four ratings must be circled after each routine, and the scale need only be completed when teachers deem it necessary.

The CEQ is a tool for developing a profile of a child's propensity for engagement, specifically competence and undifferentiated engagement. Parents or other caregivers rate 32 items. This scale is useful for determining whether the early intervention program is working. Experience has shown that most families and teachers are able to complete this successfully.

Discussion Questions

1. Define and give examples of the following:
   a. Nonengagement
   b. Unsophisticated engagement
   c. Average engagement
   d. Advanced engagement
   e. Sophisticated engagement
2. True or false? When rating the complexity of a child's engagement, the teacher should rate how the child spent the most amount of time, not the highest level of engagement observed.
3. Is your classroom staff currently aware of engagement during each routine of the day?
4. How might use of the STARE benefit your classroom as a whole? How might it benefit individual children?
5. What are the three underlying factors measured by the CEQ?
6. What is the difference between STARE engagement scores and CEQ ratings?

Notes and Ideas

Section V

Conclusion

12 *Chapter*

Putting It All Together

When summarizing the engagement approach to preschool education, it is helpful to consider 1) what it means to think about engagement when running a classroom, 2) how the Engagement Classroom (McWilliam, 2004) might be structured differently from regular classrooms, and 3) how an individual would know he or she has succeeded at establishing the Engagement Classroom.

WHAT DOES IT MEAN TO THINK ABOUT ENGAGEMENT WHEN RUNNING A CLASSROOM?

Teaching with an engagement mindset means adopting a philosophy that is at once fundamentally different from the usual teaching mindset and a good fit with constructivist, behavioral, and ecological theories. The usual mindset is often focused on having children learn skills in a curriculum—actually, it is often focused on children participating in the activities that lead them to learn those skills. With an engagement mindset, teachers are concerned about engagement in three ways. First, they want all children to be engaged at some level: Leave no child nonengaged! Second, they want individual children to spend most of their time in the classroom engaged. Third, they want individual children to increase the sophistication of their engagement. Thinking about engagement means thinking about all three of these dimensions of engagement.

Thinking about engagement also means understanding the concept of busyness. Teachers who are concerned with engagement think, "My business is children's busyness." Because not all children in a classroom have the same interests and abilities, "engagement teachers" understand that

- Some children will be more engaged with adults than peers or materials
- Some children will be more engaged with peers
- Some children will be more engaged with materials
- Some children will be more engaged with one routine, whereas other children will be more engaged with another
- Some children will be engaged at an unsophisticated level
- Other children will be engaged at a sophisticated level

Despite these differences, engagement is the unifying strand in teachers' minds. They are aiming for

- Full participation by all children
- Maximum participation by any individual child
- The most sophisticated behavior that is developmentally appropriate for an individual child

HOW IS THE ENGAGEMENT CLASSROOM STRUCTURED DIFFERENTLY FROM REGULAR CLASSROOMS?

In classrooms with children with disabilities, teachers should be concerned with those children's goals, with using supports to help children meet their goals, with providing instruction for children, and with managing adults and space in the classroom.

The first characteristic of the Engagement Classroom is having functional goals, which are defined as goals children need to participate successfully in their learning environments (home, school, and community). We recently heard a federal official with responsibility for educational research describe his purview as "schools," but this is too narrow a view when considering young children. Learning opportunities exist at home, at school, and in the community; children are learning in all those environments, whether or not adults realize it. And, if adults want children to learn as much as possible, they must ensure that their practices are relevant for all three environments. Therefore, functional goals address needs in children's regular routines. In the Engagement Classroom, assessment addresses not only children's developmental status and their ability to perform skills in the curriculum but also what they need to successfully participate in routines. These needs are assessed through a Routines-Based Interview, which produces functional goals.

A second characteristic of the Engagement Classroom is attention to how supports to the child with disabilities are provided. Traditionally, therapy services or itinerant early childhood special education has involved direct, hands-on work with a child. In the new model, the limitations of that approach are met head-on with a reconceptualization of these specialized services, and the child is not pulled out for therapy or special education. Services are extended far beyond the time of the session by having the specialists use the session to work with the child in the context of the regular classroom routines. This

- Makes specialists' suggestions relevant

- Allows specialists to see how the child functions during the many hours when a specialist is not present
- Allows specialists to learn from the classroom staff about how to interact with the child
- Allows teachers to see how the specialized interventions can be done in the context of regular routines
- Gives both teachers and specialists time to communicate

A third characteristic of the Engagement Classroom is that interventions with children with disabilities occur throughout the day; this is known as embedded intervention. Teachers generally do not need to do additional activities with these children, but they do need to pay attention to opportunities to teach throughout the regular routines. The key practice is incidental teaching, in which adults

- Provide interesting things for children to do
- Follow children's leads
- Elicit elaboration of existing behavior (i.e., scaffold) toward
    - Skills identified on the IEP
    - More time spent with the activity of interest
    - More sophisticated interaction with the person or object of interest

What differentiates incidental teaching from some other forms of responsive teaching is that the child is coaxed into elaboration of the existing behavior. Being responsive by acknowledging the child's activities or praising behavior is not enough if engagement is not affected (this is what we call a *nonelaborative response*); the teacher's responsiveness must elicit elaboration to be considered incidental teaching.

The fourth characteristic of the Engagement Classroom is the use of the zone defense schedule, which means that

- The room is organized into zones
- All adults are individually scheduled throughout the day
- Transitions between activities occur with almost no downtime

In addition to promoting greater engagement, the zone defense schedule ensures that all of the adults are used maximally. Everyone plans his or her activities, which empowers assistants. Lead teachers are resources for assistants and are still ultimately responsible. The use of the set-up role during each activity also helps to maintain at least one teacher's involvement with the children in the activity. The Engagement Classroom, therefore, differs from regular classrooms through its emphasis on functional goals, integrated therapy and consultative services, incidental teaching, and the zone defense schedule.

HOW WILL I KNOW IF I HAVE SUCCEEDED?

Teachers should have methods for determining whether they are implementing recommended practices for improving children's engagement and whether children are benefiting immediately. The main method for determining whether practices are being implemented is the use of performance checklists. These outline the steps for the practice, allowing teachers to evaluate themselves or supervisors to evaluate teachers. We encourage the frequent use of checklists to make sure the practices continue as designed.

To determine whether children are benefiting from a focus on engagement, teachers can use the Engagement Check II (McWilliam, 1999), the STARE (McWilliam, 2000), and the CEQ (McWilliam, 1991; blank forms of these assessments can be found in Appendix B). The Engagement Check II is suitable for rating classwide engagement. The STARE and CEQ are used to rate individual engagement, but whereas the STARE is suitable for rating children's engagement in specific situations (i.e., routines), the CEQ is suitable for rating children's propensity for engagement. The Engagement Check II and STARE can be scored frequently—such as weekly—whereas the CEQ is probably best scored no more often than every 3 months.

All of this attention to engagement can have three important consequences. First, engaged children are children who are competent in their environments. This means that children's quality of life and the quality of life of their caregivers is improved, compared to when children are less competent. Second, engaged children are children who know how to keep themselves busy, how to do things on their own, and how to interact with others. These characteristics are the details of competence; they have been described as the foundations for learning in a modern society (McWilliam, 2005c). Third, engaged children will, in academic environments, learn academic skills such as reading, writing, and counting. Teachers should remember, however, that academic activities in the preschool years can and should be enjoyable for children and should not look like traditional first-grade activities. In conclusion, then, teachers have succeeded when they are using engagement-promoting practices, children are measurably engaged, and children are prepared for future learning.

References

Aguiar, C. (2005, July). *Mother interaction behavior effects on child engagement.* Paper presented at the FPG Child Development Institute, University of North Carolina, Chapel Hill.

Almqvist, L. (2006). Patterns of engagement in young children with and without developmental delay. *Journal of Policy and Practice in Intellectual Disabilities, 3,* 65–75.

Berliner, D.C., & Rosenshine, B. (1977). The acquisition of knowledge in the classroom. In R. Spiro & W. Montague (Eds.), *Schooling and the acquisition of knowledge.* Mahwah, NJ: Lawrence Erlbaum Associates.

Bredekamp, S. (1987). *Developmentally appropriate practice in early childhood programs serving children from birth through age 8.* Washington, DC: National Association for the Education of Young Children.

Bredekamp, S., Knuth, R.A., Kunesh, L.G., & Shulman, D.D. (1992). *What does research say about early childhood education?* Retrieved May 29, 2005, from http://www.ncrel.org/sdrs/areas/stw_esys/5erly_ch.htm

Casey, A.M., Freund, P.J., & McWilliam, R.A. (2004). *Vanderbilt Ecological Congruence of Teaching Opportunities in Routines (VECTOR)—Classroom Version.* Nashville, TN: Vanderbilt University Medical Center, Center for Child Development.

Casey, A.M., & McWilliam, R.A. (2005). Where is everybody? Organizing adults to promote child engagement. *Young Exceptional Children, 8,* 2–10.

Casey, A.M., & McWilliam, R.A. (in press). Graphical feedback to increase teachers' use of incidental teaching. *Journal of Early Intervention.*

de Kruif, R.E.L., & McWilliam, R.A. (1999). Multivariate relationships among developmental age, global engagement, and observed child engagement. *Early Childhood Research Quarterly, 14,* 515–536.

Driscoll, C., & Carter, M. (2004). Spatial density as a setting event for the social interaction of preschool children. *International Journal of Disability, Development, and Education, 51,* 7–37.

Dunst, C.J., & McWilliam, R.A. (1988). Cognitive assessment of multiply handicapped young children. In T. Wachs & R. Sheehan (Eds.), *Assessment of developmentally disabled children* (pp. 213–238). New York: Plenum Press.

Dunst, C.J., McWilliam, R.A., & Holbert, K. (1986). Assessment of preschool classroom environments. *Diagnostique, 11,* 212–232.

Favell, J.E., Favell, J.E., Reid, D.H., & Risley, T.R. (1983, December). *Organizing living environments for developmentally disabled persons.* Workshop presentation at the World Congress on Behavior Therapy and 17th annual Association for the Advancement of Behavior Therapy Convention, Washington, DC.

Favell, J.E., & Risley, T.R. (1984, November). *Organizing living environments for developmentally disabled persons.* Workshop presentation at the 18th annual Association for the Advancement of Behavior Therapy Convention, Philadelphia, PA.

Fisher, C.W., & Berliner, D.C. (1985). *Perspectives on instructional time.* New York: Longman.

Hart, B., & Risley, T.R. (1975). Incidental teaching of language in the preschool. *Journal of Applied Behavior Analysis, 8,* 411–420.

Hart, B., & Risley, T.R. (1978). Promoting productive language through incidental teaching. *Education and Urban Society, 10,* 407–429.

Hart, B., & Risley, T.R. (1980). In vivo language intervention: Unanticipated general effects. *Journal of Applied Behavior Analysis, 13,* 407–432.

Individuals with Disabilities Education Act Amendments of 1997, PL 105-17, 20 U.S.C. §§ 1400 *et seq.*

Individuals with Disabilities Education Improvement Act of 2004, PL 108-446, 20 U.S.C. §§ 1400 *et seq.*

Jennings, K.D. (2004). Development of goal-directed behavior and related self-processes in toddlers. *International Journal of Behavioral Development, 28,* 319–327.

Krantz, P.J., & Risley, T.R. (1977). Behavioral ecology in the classroom. In K.D. O'Leary & S.G. O'Leary (Eds.), *Classroom management: The successful use of behavior modification* (2nd ed., pp. 349–367). New York: Pergamon Press.

Leavitt, R.L., & Eheart, B.K. (1985). *Toddler day care: A guide to responsive caregiving.* Lexington, MA: Lexington Books.

LeLaurin, K., & Risley, T.R. (1972). The organization of daycare environments: "Zone" versus "man-to-man" staff assignments. *Journal of Applied Behavior Analysis, 5,* 225–232.

McEwan, M.H., Dihoff, R.E., & Brosvic, G.M. (1991). Early infant crawling experience is reflected in later motor skill development. *Perceptual Motor Skills, 72,* 75–79.

McGee, G.G., Daly, T., Izeman, S.G., Mann, L.H., & Risley, T.R. (1991). Use of classroom materials to promote preschool engagement. *Teaching Exceptional Children, 23,* 44–47.

McWilliam, R.A. (1991). *Children's Engagement Questionnaire (CEQ).* Chapel Hill: University of North Carolina, FPG Child Development Institute.

McWilliam, R.A. (1992a). *Family-centered intervention planning: A routines-based approach.* Tucson, AZ: Communication Skill Builders.

McWilliam, R.A. (1992b). *The Intervention Matrix.* Chapel Hill: University of North Carolina, FPG Child Development Institute.

McWilliam, R.A. (1995). Integration of therapy and consultative special education: A continuum in early intervention. *Infants and Young Children, 7*(4), 29–38.

McWilliam, R.A. (1996a). A program of research on integrated versus isolated treatment in early intervention. In R.A. McWilliam (Ed.), *Rethinking pull-out services in early intervention: A professional resource* (pp. 49–69). Baltimore: Paul H. Brookes Publishing Co.

McWilliam, R.A. (Ed.). (1996b). Rethinking pull-out services in early intervention: A professional resource. Baltimore: Paul H. Brookes Publishing Co.

McWilliam, R.A. (1999). *Engagement Check II.* Chapel Hill: University of North Carolina, FPG Child Development Institute.

McWilliam, R.A. (2000). *Scale for Teachers' Assessment of Routines Engagement* (STARE). Chapel Hill: University of North Carolina, FPG Child Development Institute.

McWilliam, R.A. (2002). *Zone defense scheduling template.* Nashville: Vanderbilt University Medical Center, Center for Child Development.

McWilliam, R.A. (2004). *The Engagement Classroom: A model for preschool inclusion.* Grant No. H324C040114 awarded to Vanderbilt University Medical Center by the U.S. Department of Education, Office of Special Education Programs, Washington, DC.

McWilliam, R.A. (2005a). Assessing the resource needs of families in the context of early intervention. In M.J. Guralnick (Ed.), *The developmental systems approach to early intervention* (pp. 215–233). Baltimore: Paul H. Brookes Publishing Co.

McWilliam, R.A. (2005b, March). *Family variables in a diagnostic clinic.* Paper presented at the Pediatric Research Conference, Department of Pediatrics, Vanderbilt University School of Medicine, Nashville, TN.

McWilliam, R.A. (2005c, May). Foundations for learning in a modern society. Paper presented at the Encontro Internacional Diferenciação do Conceito à Práctica, Universidade Católica Portuguesa, Porto, Portugal.

McWilliam, R.A. (2005d). *Goal Functionality Scale.* Nashville: Vanderbilt University Medical Center, Center for Child Development.

McWilliam, R.A. (2005e). *Incidental Teaching Checklist.* Nashville: Vanderbilt University Medical Center, Center for Child Development.

McWilliam, R.A. (2005f). *Zone Defense Schedule Implementation Checklist.* Nashville: Vanderbilt University Medical Center, Center for Child Development.

McWilliam, R.A., & Bailey, D.B. (1992). Promoting engagement and mastery. In D.B. Bailey & M. Wolery (Eds.), *Teaching infants and toddlers with disabilities* (2nd ed., pp. 229–256). New York: Merrill.

McWilliam, R.A., & Bailey, D.B. (1995). Effects of classroom social structure and disability on engagement. *Topics in Early Childhood Special Education, 15,* 123–147.

McWilliam, R.A., & Casey, A.M. (2004). *Engagement Quality and Incidental Teaching for Improved Education (E-Qual-ITIE).* Nashville: Vanderbilt University Medical Center, Center for Child Development.

McWilliam, R.A., & de Kruif, R.E.L. (1998). *E-Qual III: Children's engagement codes.* Chapel Hill: University of North Carolina, FPG Child Development Institute.

McWilliam, R.A., de Kruif, R.E.L., & Zulli, R.A. (2002). The observed construction of teaching: Four contexts. *Journal of Research in Childhood Education, 16,* 148–161.

McWilliam, R.A., & Scott, S. (2001). *Examination of the Implementation of Embedded Intervention, through Observation* (EIEIO). Chapel Hill: University of North Carolina, FPG Child Development Institute.

McWilliam, R.A., Trivette, C.M., & Dunst, C.J. (1985). Behavior engagement as a measure of the efficacy of early intervention. *Analysis and Intervention in Developmental Disabilities, 5,* 59–71.

O'Brien, M. (1997). *Inclusive child care for infants and toddlers: Meeting individual and special needs.* Baltimore: Paul H. Brookes Publishing Co.

Parten, M.B. (1932). Social participation among pre-school children. *Journal of Abnormal and Social Psychology, 27,* 243–269.

Rasmussen, J.L., & McWilliam, R.A. (2006). *RBI Implementation Checklist.* Nashville: Vanderbilt University Medical Center, Center for Child Development.

Ridley, S.M., & McWilliam, R.A. (2001). Putting the child back into child care quality assessment. *Young Children, 56*(4), 92–93.

Risley, R.R., & Cataldo, M.F. (1973). *Planned activity check: Materials for training observers.* Lawrence, KS: Center for Applied Behavior Analysis.

Sainato, D.M., Strain, P.S., Lefebvre, D., & Rapp, N. (1987). Facilitating transition times with handicapped preschool children: A comparison between peer-mediated and antecedent prompt procedures. *Journal of Applied Behavior Analysis, 20,* 285–291.

Sandall, S., McLean, M.E., & Smith, B.J. (2000). *DEC recommended practices in early intervention/early childhood special education.* Reston, VA: Council for Exceptional Children, Division for Early Childhood.

Schank, R.C., & Cleary, C. (1995). *Engines for education.* Mahwah, NJ: Lawrence Erlbaum Associates.

Snyder, P., & McWilliam, R.A. (2005). *Ratings of child engagement.* Manuscript in preparation.

Snyder, P., & McWilliam, R.A. (2006, March). *Using parallel analysis to inform extraction decisions in factor analysis: Application with the Children's Engagement Questionnaire.* Poster presented at the Conference on Research Innovations in Early Intervention, San Diego.

Stokes, T.F., & Baer, D.M. (1977). An implicit technology of generalization. *Journal of Applied Behavior Analysis, 10,* 349–367.

Thurman, S.K. (1997). Systems, ecologies, and the context of early intervention. In S.K. Thurman, J.R. Cornwell, & S.R. Gottwald (Eds.), *Contexts of early intervention: Systems and settings* (pp. 3–17). Baltimore: Paul H. Brookes Publishing Co.

VanDerHeyden, A.M., Snyder, P., Smith, A., Sevin, B., & Longwell, J. (2005). Effects of complete learning trials on child engagement. *Topics in Early Childhood Special Education, 25,* 81–94.

Vygotsky, L.S. (1978). *Mind in society: The development of higher mental processes* (M. Cole, V. John-Steiner, S. Scribner, & E. Souberman, Eds.). Cambridge, MA: Harvard University Press. (Original work published 1930, 1933, 1935)

Wolery, M., Anthony, L., Caldwell, N.K., Snyder, E.D., & Morgante, J.D. (2002). Embedding and distributing constant time delay in circle time and transitions. *Topics in Early Childhood Special Education, 22,* 14–25.

Wolery, M., Brashers, M.S., & Neitzel, J.C. (2002). Ecological congruence assessment for classroom activities and routines: Identifying goals and intervention practices in childcare. *Topics in Early Childhood Special Education, 22,* 131–142.

Wolery, M., Strain, P.S., & Bailey, D.B. (1992). Applying the framework of developmentally appropriate practice to children with special needs. In S. Bredekamp & T. Rosegrant (Eds.), *Reaching potentials: Curriculum and assessment for 3 to 8 year olds* (pp. 92–113). Washington, DC: National Association for the Education of Young Children.

The Engagement Construct

R.A. McWILLIAM

The purpose of this appendix is to present the definition of engagement as we use it in the book, to reveal its roots, to discuss serendipitous theoretical connections, and to suggest that it forms a unified theory of practice. The need for such a treatment of the construct has been revealed most unmistakably in Europe (Aguiar, Cruz, Barros, & Bairrão, 2005; Almqvist & Granlund, 2005), where theory is of paramount concern.

CURRENT DEFINITION

Engagement is a construct that today is applied to all children, with a special application for children with disabilities. It is defined as *the amount of time a child spends interacting with the environment in a developmentally and contextually appropriate manner at different levels of competence;* this definition has existed essentially as such for 15 years (McWilliam & Bailey, 1992). It is about duration of behavior in context, not about performance of isolated tasks in a testing situation. Interactions can vary in sophistication, from nonengaged through unsophisticated behavior to sophisticated behavior. Most of the work using this definition has been conducted with children from birth through 5 years old. As seen in Figure A.1, most time in early childhood classrooms is spent in differentiated engagement, which is like a default category—behavior that is neither undifferentiated nor sophisticated. The next category accounting for time spent is attentional behavior: watching and listening. Typically, sophisticated engagement and nonengagement are the least common categories, but the environment certainly makes a difference. For example, in Portuguese studies (Pinto, 2006; see Figure A.2), less focused attention and more nonengagement were seen than in the five studies depicted in Figure A.1.

Interactions with the environment can be passive or active, but active engagement is considered more developmentally advantageous and sophisticated. A child who is thinking and concentrating on a problem would, in this observational paradigm, be considered passively nonengaged, even though such mental behavior might be considered sophisticated. From a behavioral standpoint, however, we can only guess what is going on inside the child's head. This is the first clue that engagement is fundamentally a behavioral construct; it is about observable

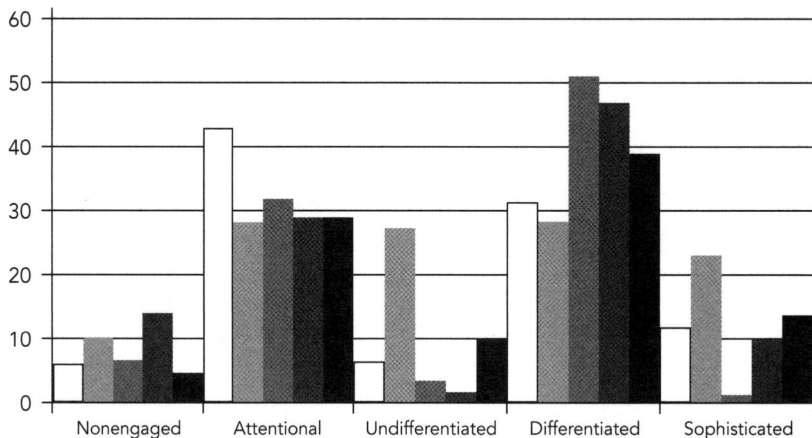

Figure A.1. Engagement levels from five studies. (*Key:* □ McWilliam & Ware, 1994; ■ McWilliam & Bailey, 1995; ■ de Kruif & McWilliam, 1999; ■ McWilliam, Scarborough, & Kim, 2003; ■ Raspa, McWilliam, & Ridley, 2001.)

and therefore measurable behavior. Young children, fortunately, do not spend much time just thinking; they quickly act on what we assume are their thoughts.

The dimensions of the environment that children interact with when they are engaged can be classified as adults, peers, and materials. The last dimension includes space so that children in motion are classified as engaged with materials. But this is where some inference is made. If we can tell what a child is moving toward, we classify that movement in terms of the child's goal. For example, if a child sees his or her mother enter the room and starts moving toward her, the amount of time spent in that movement is considered engagement with an adult—the child's mother. If, however, a child is running around the playground, not involved in a social game, the behavior would be considered engagement with materials. Occasionally, we acknowledge children's engagement with self, when they are fussing with their own clothing, for example. Usually, such behavior is nonengagement. Most behaviors of young children can be classified as relating to adults, peers, or materials.

Engagement is an exhaustive construct. Unlike the similar construct of involvement (Laevers, n.d.), which is related to specific contexts and situations, engagement is now a construct that applies to all behavior. Hence, it is classified by type (adults, peers, materials), level (sophistication classifications), and amount. To understand the construct, it is critical to recognize all three dimensions (see Figure A.3).

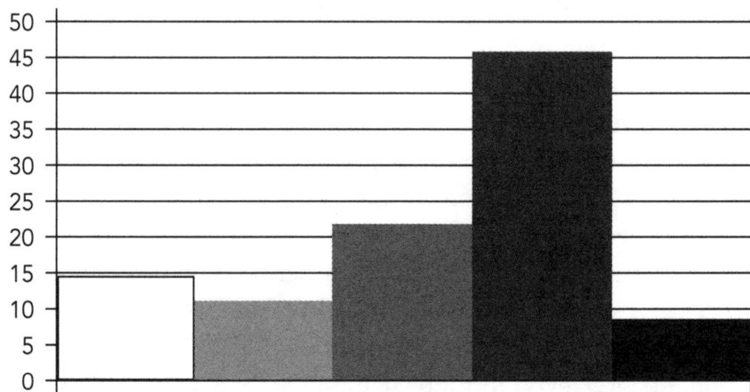

Figure A.2. Portuguese study distribution of engagement categories (*Source:* Pinto, 2006. (*Key:* □ Nonengagement, ■ Unsophisticated engagement, ■ Focused attention, ■ Differentiated, ■ Sophisticated engagement.)

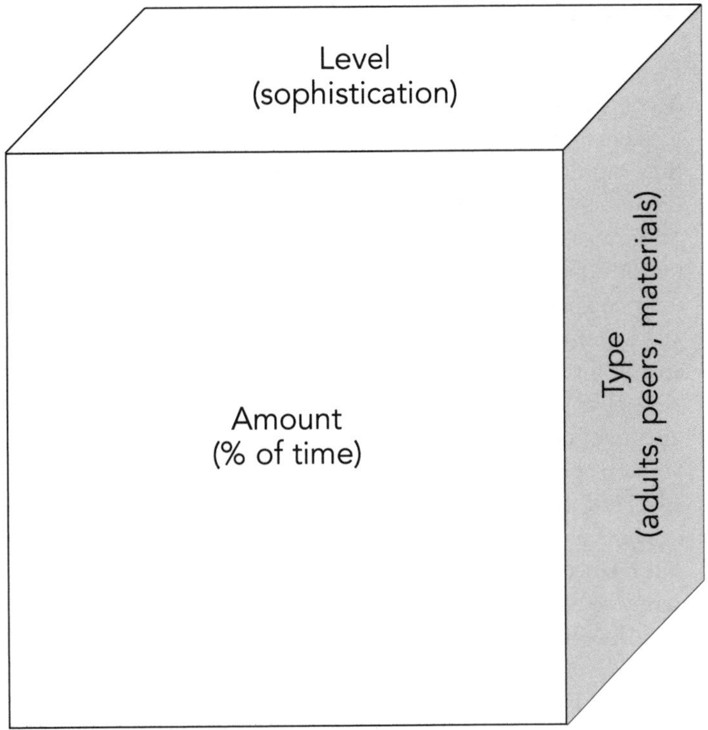

Figure A.3. The three dimensions of engagement.

Appropriateness is a very important aspect of engagement. The two main types of appropriateness considered are developmental and contextual. To be considered engaged, the child must display a behavior one would expect to be appropriate for his or her developmental, not chronological, level. Furthermore, it must be acceptable behavior for the context. Otherwise, the behavior is considered nonengaged or, sometimes, engaged at a low level.

The different levels of competence are a hallmark of the work of our laboratories at the University of North Carolina (UNC) and Vanderbilt University. Before our research, engagement had been considered a dichotomous variable—engaged or not. We currently conceptualize engagement in the three types (adults, peers, materials) as occurring at nine levels, which we usually then reduce to five categories, as seen in Figure A.4.

Levels	Categories
1. Persistence 2. Symbolic 3. Encoded 4. Constructive	Sophisticated
5. Differentiated 6. Focused attention	Differentiated/Participation Focused Attention
7. Undifferentiated 8. Causal attention	Unsophisticated
9. Nonengagement	Nonengaged

Sophistication (↑)

Figure A.4. Levels and categories of engagement.

The E-I-SR Framework

Engagement can be considered one of the three foundations of learning, along with independence and social relationships (McWilliam, 2006). These three aspects of child functioning are the core of the child-level questions in the Routines-Based Interview (McWilliam, 2005) because they capture most needs for successful child behavior in routines. Consequently, functional intervention plans largely consist of goals in these three areas, in addition to parent-level goals. These areas are preferable to the traditional domains of development (e.g., cognitive, language, motor, adaptive, social) for a number of reasons. First, the foundations of learning are holistic; they do not divide child functioning into functioning largely related to the body: cognitive, related to the head; motor, related to the arms and legs; communication, related to the mouth; and so forth. Second, the foundations are cross-disciplinary, whereas the traditional domains have each come to be associated with different specialty disciplines: cognitive with psychologists or educators, communication with speech-language pathologists, and motor with occupational or physical therapists. The modern approach to early intervention finds such domain-specialty matching simplistic. Preferably, specialists such as therapists help families and teachers with whole-child functioning, which the triad of engagement, independence, and social relationships (often designated *E-I-SR*) promotes. Third, E-I-SR is a framework that cuts across routines, types of children, and types of families, with the caveats noted next.

In every routine, we can ask what a child's participation (engagement) is like: to what extent and at what level of sophistication he or she participates in the routine. In every routine, we can ask what a child's independence is like: to what extent he or she can do the tasks of the routine independently. In every routine, we can also ask what a child's social relationships are like: to what extent he or she communicates and gets along with others.

Engagement has been defined previously. Independence is self-explanatory, but it should be noted that different cultural groups have different values when it comes to young children's independence. Some groups believe it is the mother's role to do things for her child at least until school age, whereas other groups believe the child should be independent yet compliant at an early age. Early childhood professionals, therefore, are encouraged to be sensitive to the cultural and individual beliefs of families.

Social relationships consist of communicating and getting along with others. According to Shonkoff and Phillips (2000), social and emotional well-being is critical for learning. We argue that they are also critical for a good quality of life. E-I-SR is, therefore, a useful framework for assessing children's needs and planning interventions. It might not replace traditional curricular areas such as literacy and numeracy, but it works for all children, regardless of age or cognitive level, and it is probably a foundation for achievement in such areas. That is, engagement, independence, and social relationships might not be sufficient but are probably necessary.

Relevance of the E-I-SR Framework for Children with Disabilities

The E-I-SR framework has been mentioned in the context of all children, but it has particular relevance for children with disabilities. Almost by definition, developmental and sensory disabilities can interfere with a child's engagement, independence, and social relationships. Focusing intervention on these areas can therefore be efficacious, but it can also promote strengths in child functioning. As specialists and caregivers (i.e., family members, teachers) assess functioning in routines in these areas, strengths in participation (engagement), independence, and social relationships are as likely to be identified as are weaknesses. By concentrating on functioning in routines, goals can be ecologically relevant, which is helpful for learning by the child and implementation of the interventions by the adult. This means that adults are more likely to carry out strategies for which they can see the environmental relevance, and children are more likely to learn when they are taught in context. The three foundations of learning release specialists, families, and children from the shackles of traditional domains and decontextualized goals.

Engagement has evolved in three stages: the roots of our own work, similar constructs, and serendipitous theoretical connections.

STAGE 1: ROOTS

Engagement is commonly viewed as either inherently commonsensical (Bailey & Wolery, 1992) or as alien (according to reviews of engagement research in certain child development journals). Both reactions expose the need for an explanation of its roots; people who view it as common sense can attach it to numerous theories and traditions, whereas people who do not understand it want to know where it came from and how it is different from play, competence, temperament, and so forth. The explanation given here refers solely to the form of engagement studied in the labs at UNC and Vanderbilt and in their offshoots, such as the University of Porto in Portugal. Other conceptualizations of engagement (e.g., Connell, Spencer, & Aber, 1994; Dishion, Duncan, Eddy, Fagot, & Fetrow, 1994; Lewy & Dawson, 1992) might have different roots.

Our first exposure to engagement came from Todd Risley, who in the 1970s at the University of Kansas pioneered the concept of counting the percentage of people participating in planned activities, averaged across multiple frequent observations. With Mike Cataldo, the Planned Learning Activities (PLA) Check was developed to determine this "group engagement" in settings for toddlers and preschoolers (Risley & Cataldo, 1973). Carl Dunst was the person who incorporated Risley's engagement work in Project SUNRISE, a model demonstration and outreach project showing the benefits of parent-run, inclusive co-ops for meeting the developmental needs of infants, toddlers, and preschoolers with disabilities (McWilliam, Trivette, & Dunst, 1985). Risley's background is in operant conditioning applied in real-life contexts. Engagement was viewed as the behavior resulting from environments that set the occasion for desired behavior; it was also viewed as a behavior that set the occasion for incidental teaching (Hart & Risley, 1978). Thus, the cycle of incidental teaching and engagement, which is still a major component of our work (Casey & McWilliam, 2007), was present from the beginning. The behavioral and ecological roots are fundamental to the engagement construct.

Dunst applied his interest in stages of cognitive development, influenced by the work of Uzgiris and Hunt (1975), to the engagement construct. In 1988, a process for assessing cognitive functioning, called the OBSERVE (Dunst & McWilliam, 1988), married engagement and stages of cognitive development. Dunst was instrumental in shaping this line of work to straddle more than one theoretical home. Thus, although the roots Risley planted were clearly behavioral, a graft with developmental roots was to prove possible.

Other researchers interested in the engagement of young children with disabilities beginning in the early 1980s were Charlie Greenwood (1991), Judy Carta (Carta, Sainato, & Greenwood, 1988), and Sam Odom (1988). Their emphasis was on measuring the amount of time children spent in different activities in preschool classrooms, and their measurement systems captured many different aspects of the ecology.

STAGE 2: DISCOVERING SIMILAR CONSTRUCTS

As writings evolved, the literature was combed and a number of similar concepts were found. It should be noted that these similar concepts were not, then, the original roots in our work, but they did influence refinement of the construct. Early on, we found that Fisher and Berliner's (1985) work on teacher effectiveness had used time on task as a mediator, or at least moderator, of the effects of teaching competence on student achievement in school-age children. They described how time was apportioned in schools, as shown in Figure A.5.

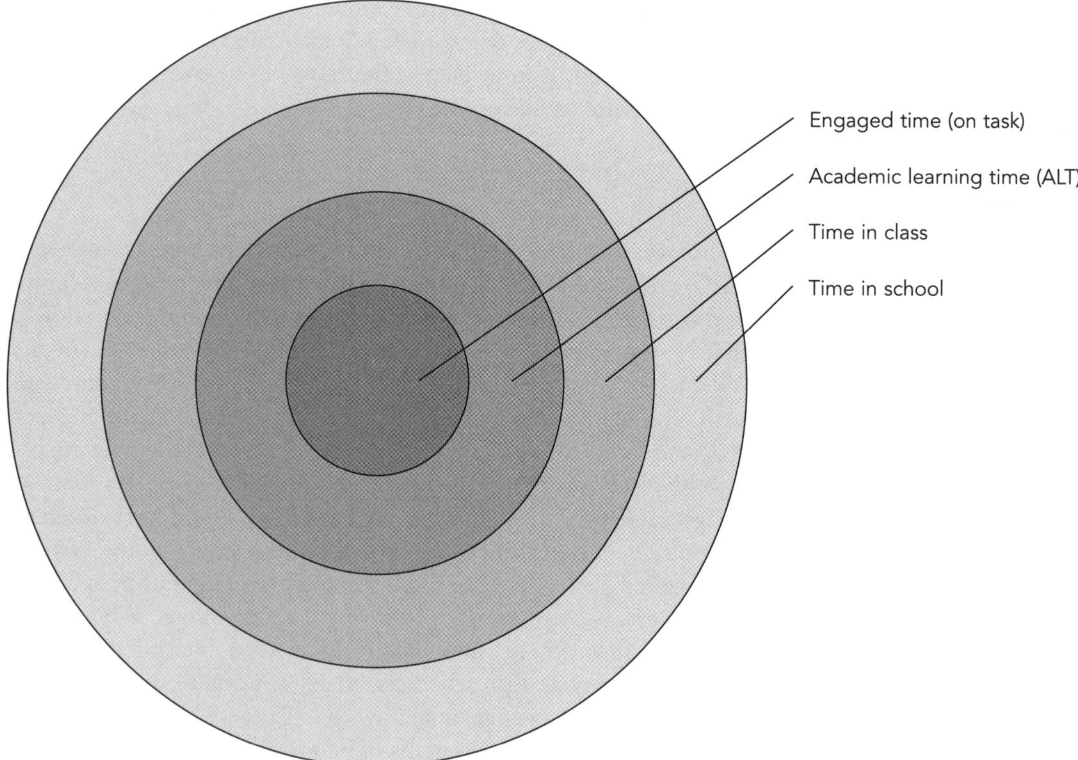

Figure A.5. How time is apportioned in schools (*Source:* Fisher & Berliner, 1985).

Only a portion of the time children are in school are they in class, only a portion of the time they are in class are they involved in academic learning tasks, and only a portion of the time they are involved in academic learning tasks are they actually engaged or on task. Thinking about school-age applications of time spent on task allowed us to consider a couple of important differences between that and engagement. First, all time "in school" was considered learning time. As Dunst and colleagues (Dunst, Hamby, Trivette, Raab, & Bruder, 2000) were later to operationalize, "learning opportunities" abound wherever children are. Second, what is not "on task" for a young child, where play and other informal interactions are the stuff of learning? Therefore, a child did not have to be involved in some formal learning activity to be considered engaged. One of the real benefits of learning about the teacher effectiveness research was to understand the importance of how children spend their time (Fisher & Berliner, 1985).

A pioneer of the research on the importance of time spent was John Carroll (1963), whose model of school learning was based on his findings that the time students spent studying a set of skills (e.g., a foreign language) was related to learning those skills. A side note is that when Professor Emeritus John Carroll (UNC-Chapel Hill) was told that his work was iconoclastic in the construct of engagement in young children, 25 years after his work was published, he had no idea.

As work continued on methods of conceptualizing and measuring the quality of a child's engagement, parallels with White's (1959) mastery motivation became clear. In this theory, children are motivated to master tasks (Kelley, Brownell, & Campbell, 2000; MacTurk, Hunter, McCarthy, Vietze, & McQuiston, 1985; Yarrow et al., 1983). More pertinent to the engagement work was Morgan and Harmon's subsequent theory of mastery behavior (Blasco, Bailey, & Burchinal, 1993; Brockman, Morgan, & Harmon, 1988; Bronson, Hauser-Cram, & Warfield, 1997; Hauser-Cram, 1996; Messer, Rachford, McCarthy, & Yarrow, 1987; Morgan, Harmon, & Maslin-Cole, 1990), in which goal directedness could be seen as a more sophisticated level of engagement with adults, peers, and materials than nonmastery engagement, in which a child interacted with the environment for no observable purpose (McWilliam & Bailey, 1992). This way of measuring engagement was used in one engagement study (McWilliam & Ware, 1994). One problem, however, was that inference was needed to determine whether a child was goal directed, which made reliable measurement difficult, although we did eventually manage to do it.

STAGE 3: SERENDIPITOUS THEORETICAL CONNECTIONS

Because much of our work is in early intervention and early childhood special education, where reference to Bronfenbrenner's (1979) ecological framework is boundless, it became apparent that engagement, which is about behavior in context, was clearly aligned with this framework. From the beginning, Risley and colleagues were interested in group engagement and in language teaching in naturalistic environments. As other language researchers placed incidental teaching in an intervention class they called milieu teaching, they framed their approach as behavioral–ecological (Warren & Kaiser, 1986, 1988). The ecological framework as conceptualized by Bronfenbrenner and the similar structural/behavioral model of development as conceptualized by Horowitz (1987) were discovered to be comfortable homes for engagement, even if engagement did not actually emerge from them.

As Vygotsky's (1978) zone of proximal development became familiar to Americans and Europeans in the late 20th and early 21st centuries, the application of engagement to this notion seemed to be a good fit. Vygotsky was interested in methods to promote children's competence, which complements the levels of sophistication in engagement. The fact that this early constructivist way of thinking about children's development was a far cry from Skinner's (1953), who was Risley's guru, did not make it irrelevant. After all, Vygotsky had influenced the stage theorists such as Piaget (1954), and the early roots of engagement were found in Uzgiris and Hunt (1975), followed by Dunst (1981). Furthermore, work with engagement of young children with disabilities has demonstrated the importance of active versus passive engagement (Dunst, McWilliam, & Holbert, 1986), which is consistent with other constructivists such as Dewey (1925), who favored learning through doing. Current students of engagement appear to gravitate toward the theoretical backgrounds familiar to them; thus, Portuguese early childhood researchers tend to concentrate on the Russian and European developmental roots, whereas American special education researchers tend to concentrate on the American behavioral roots.

The latest happy discovery of a theoretical connection has been the World Health Organization's emphasis on participation as a descriptor of functioning in the classification of people with disabilities. Rune Simeonsson (Simeonsson et al., 2003), a key player in the development of the International Classification of Functioning for Children and Youth, was a professor and colleague of mine at UNC–Chapel Hill. Learning from him, it became increasingly clear to me that engagement could be considered participation in very young children. In this framework, an impairment is the abnormal condition that might or might not impede functioning, depending on a host of factors, including the extent to which the environment provides supports to the individual. One can understand the concept of participation for adults and older children as it applies to home, school, community, and work. What about young children? For them, participation can be considered engagement in their home and school—whether child care or preschool—routines. Just as it is a matter of quality of life for adults to ensure that they can participate to the extent they want to, so is it for young children—to the extent they and their families want them to. Perhaps not so strangely, this brings us full circle to Risley (1986), who delivered a paper at the Association for Behavior Analysis convention on "Behavioral Engagement as a Fundamental Variable in Treatment Quality," in which he argued that people in others' care have the right to an engaging environment.

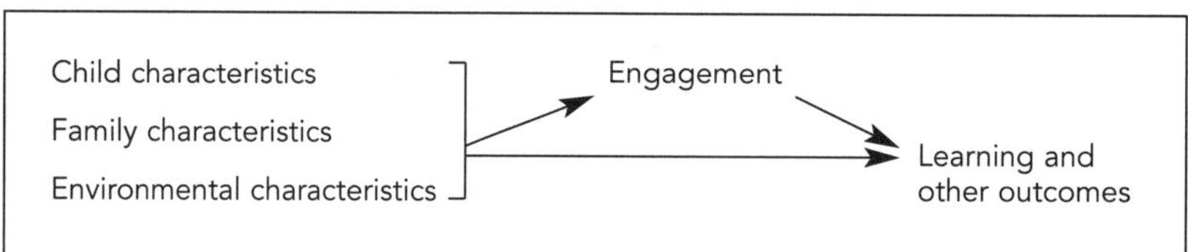

Figure A.6. The role of engagement in mediating background characteristics on child outcomes.

UNIFIED THEORY OF PRACTICE

What should be done with this smorgasbord of theories? One approach could be to latch on to one and ignore the others. This might not be bad advice for doctoral students. Most writers, however, cannot help describing the eclectic tentacles of engagement. As Pinto (2006) has argued, it might be a "unified theory of practice," which Odom and Wolery (2003) described as a method of intervention, emerging from a number of theoretical perspectives that then constitutes a theory with its own body of research and convergence of beliefs. In this theory of practice, engagement is postulated to be a key dimension in children's functioning that mediates, or at least moderates, the effects of child, family, and environmental characteristics on learning and other developmental outcomes (e.g., achievement in reading, writing, and mathematics), as shown in Figure A.6. There now appears to be enough evidence to support the engagement theory.

REFERENCES

Aguiar, C., Cruz, O., Barros, S., & Bairrão, J. (2005). Perfis interactivos maternos e envolvimento das crianças em contexto de creche. In J. Bairrão (Org.), *Desenvolvimento: contextos familiares e educativos* (pp. 74–97). Porto: LivPsi/Legis.

Almqvist, L., & Granlund, M. (2005). Participation in school environment of children and youth with disabilities: A person-oriented approach. *Scandinavian Journal of Psychology, 46,* 305–314.

Bailey, D.B., & Wolery, M. (Eds.). (1992). *Teaching infants and preschoolers with disabilities.* (2nd ed.). Columbus, OH: Merrill.

Blasco, P.M., Bailey, D.B., & Burchinal, M.A. (1993). Dimensions of mastery in same-age and mixed-age integrated classrooms. *Early Childhood Research Quarterly, 8,* 193–206.

Brockman, L.M., Morgan, G.A., & Harmon, R.J. (1988). Mastery motivation and developmental delay. In T.D. Wachs & R. Sheehan (Eds.), *Assessment of young developmentally disabled children* (pp. 321–346). New York: Plenum Press.

Bronfenbrenner, U. (1979). *The ecology of human development.* Cambridge, MA: Harvard University Press.

Bronson, M.B., Hauser-Cram, P., & Warfield, M.J. (1997). Classrooms matter: Relations between the classroom environment and the social and mastery behavior of five-year-old children with disabilities. *Journal of Applied Developmental Psychology, 18,* 331–348.

Carroll, J.B. (1963). A model of school learning. *Teachers College Record, 64,* 723–733.

Carta, J.J., Sainato, D.M., & Greenwood, C.R. (1988). Advances in the ecological assessment of classroom instruction for young children with handicaps. In S.L. Odom & M.B. Karnes (Eds.), *Early intervention for infants and children with handicaps* (pp. 217–240). Baltimore: Paul H. Brookes Publishing Co.

Casey, A.M., & McWilliam, R.A. (2007, April). *Data-based feedback to increase teachers' use of incidental teaching.* Presented at the research session at the convention of the Council for Exceptional Children, Louisville, KY.

Connell, J.P., Spencer, M.B., & Aber, J.L. (1994). Educational risk and resilience in African-American youth: Context, self, action, and outcomes in school. *Child Development, 65,* 493–506.

de Kruif, R.E.L., & McWilliam, R.A. (1999). Multivariate relationships among developmental age, global engagement, and observed child engagement. *Early Childhood Research Quarterly, 14,* 515–536.

Dewey, J. (1925). *Experience and nature.* Chicago: Open Court.

Dishion, T.J., Duncan, T.E., Eddy, J.M., Fagot, B.I., & Fetrow, R. (1994). The world of parents and peers: Coercive exchanges and children's social adaptation. *Social Development, 3,* 255–268.

Dunst, C.J. (1981). *Infant learning.* Hingham, MA: Teaching Resources.

Dunst, C.J., Hamby, D., Trivette, C.M., Raab, M., & Bruder, M.B. (2000). Everyday family and community life and children's naturally occurring learning opportunities. *Journal of Early Intervention, 23,* 151–164.

Dunst, C.J., & McWilliam, R.A. (1988). Cognitive assessment of multiply handicapped young children. In T. Wachs & R. Sheehan (Eds.), *Assessment of developmentally disabled children* (pp. 213–238). New York: Plenum.

Dunst, C.J., McWilliam, R.A., & Holbert, K. (1986). Assessment of preschool classroom environments. *Diagnostique, 11,* 212–232.

Fisher, C.W., & Berliner, D.C. (1985). *Perspectives on instructional time.* New York: Longman.

Greenwood, C.R. (1991). Longitudinal analysis of time, engagement, and achievement in at-risk versus non-risk students. *Exceptional Children, 57,* 521–535.

Hart, B., & Risley, T.R. (1978). Promoting productive language through incidental teaching. *Education and Urban Society, 10,* 407–429.

Hauser-Cram, P. (1996). Mastery motivation in toddlers with developmental disabilities. *Child Development, 67,* 236–248.

Horowitz, F.D. (1987). *Exploring developmental theories: Toward a structural/behavioral model of development.* Mahwah, NJ: Lawrence Erlbaum Associates.

Kelley, S.A., Brownell, C.A., & Campbell, S.B. (2000). Mastery motivation and self-evaluative affect in toddlers: Longitudinal relations with maternal behavior. *Child Development, 71,* 1061–1071.

Laevers, F. (n.d.). *The project Experiential Education: Concepts and experiences at the level of context, process, and outcome.* Unpublished manuscript, Katholieke Universiteit Leuven, Centre for Experiential Education.

Lewy, A.L., & Dawson, G. (1992). Social stimulation and joint attention in young autistic children. *Journal of Abnormal Child Psychology, 20,* 555–566.

MacTurk, R.H., Hunter, F.T., McCarthy, M.E., Vietze, P.M., & McQuiston, S. (1985). Social mastery motivation in Down syndrome and nondelayed infants. *Topics in Early Childhood Special Education, 4*(4), 93–109.

McWilliam, R.A. (2005). Assessing the resource needs of families in the context of early intervention. In M.J. Guralnick (Ed.), *The developmental systems approach to early intervention* (pp. 215–233). Baltimore: Paul H. Brookes Publishing Co.

McWilliam, R.A. (2006, November). *The three foundations for learning for children birth to 6 years of age* and *The missing assessment: Needs of children and families in everyday life.* Papers presented at the V Congreso Nacional de Interventcão Precoce, Associacão Nacional de Interventcão Precoce, Aveiro, Portugal.

McWilliam, R.A., & Bailey, D.B. (1992). Promoting engagement and mastery. In D.B. Bailey & M. Wolery (Eds.), *Teaching infants and preschoolers with disabilities* (2nd ed., pp. 230–255). New York: MacMillan.

McWilliam, R.A., & Bailey, D.B. (1995). Effects of classroom social structure and disability on engagement. *Topics in Early Childhood Special Education, 15,* 123–147.

McWilliam, R.A., Scarborough, A.A., & Kim, H. (2003). Adult interactions and child engagement. *Early Education and Development, 14,* 7–27.

McWilliam, R.A., Trivette, C.M., & Dunst, C.J. (1985). Behavior engagement as a measure of the efficacy of early intervention. *Analysis and Intervention in Developmental Disabilities, 5,* 33–45.

McWilliam, R.A., & Ware, W.B. (1994). The reliability of observations of young children's engagement: An application of generalizability theory. *Journal of Early Intervention, 18,* 34–47.

Messer, D.J., Rachford, D., McCarthy, M.E., & Yarrow, L.J. (1987). Assessment of mastery behavior at 30 months: Analysis of task-directed activities. *Developmental Psychology, 23,* 771–781.

Morgan, G.A., Harmon, R.J., & Maslin-Cole, C.A. (1990). Mastery motivation: Definition and measurement. *Early Education and Development, 1,* 318–339.

Odom, S.L. (1988). Research in early childhood special education: Methodologies and paradigms. In S.L. Odom & M.B. Karnes (Eds.), *Early intervention for infants and children with handicaps* (pp. 1–21). Baltimore: Paul H. Brookes Publishing Co.

Odom, S.L., & Wolery, M. (2003). A unified theory of practice in early intervention/early childhood special education: Evidence-based practices. *The Journal of Special Education, 37,* 164–173.

Piaget, J. (1954). *The construction of reality in the child* (M. Cook, Trans.). New York: Basic Books.

Pinto, A.I.M.C. (2006). *Child engagement in child care: Effects of child characteristics, context quality and teacher interactions on children's observed engagement.* Unpublished doctoral dissertation, Faculty of Psychology and Educational Sciences, University of Porto, Porto, Portugal.

Raspa, M.J., McWilliam, R.A., & Ridley, S.M. (2001). Child care quality and children's engagement. *Early Education and Development, 12,* 209–224.

Risley, T.R. (1986). *Behavioral engagement as a fundamental variable in treatment quality.* Paper presented at the Association for Behavior Analysis Twelfth Annual Convention, Milwaukee, WI.

Risley, T.R., & Cataldo, M.F. (1973). *Planned activity check: Materials for training observers* (training manual). Lawrence, KS: Center for Applied Behavior Analysis.

Shonkoff, J.P., & Phillips, D.A. (2000). *From neurons to neighborhoods. The science of early childhood development.* Washington, DC: The National Academies Press.

Simeonsson, R.J., Leonardi, M., Lollar, D., Bjorck-Akesson, E., Hollenweger, J., & Martinuzzi, A. (2003). Applying the international classification of functioning, disability and health (ICF) to measure childhood disability. *Disability and Rehabilitation, 25,* 602–610.

Skinner, B.F. (1953). *Science and human behavior.* New York: Macmillan.

Uzgiris, I., & Hunt, J.M. (1975). *Assessment in infancy.* Urbana: University of Illinois Press.

Vygotsky, L.S. (1978). *Mind in society: The development of higher mental processes* (M. Cole, V. John-Steiner, S. Scribner, & E. Souberman, Eds.). Cambridge, MA: Harvard University Press. (Original work published 1930, 1933, 1935)

Warren, S.F., & Kaiser, A.P. (1986). Incidental language teaching: A critical view. *Journal of Speech and Hearing Disorders, 51,* 291–298.

Warren, S.F., & Kaiser, A.P. (1988). Research in early language intervention. In S.L. Odom & M.B. Karnes (Eds.), *Early intervention for infants and children with handicaps: An empirical base* (pp. 89–108). Baltimore: Paul H. Brookes Publishing Co.

White, R.W. (1959). Motivation reconsidered: The concept of competence. *Psychological Review, 66,* 297–333.

Yarrow, L.J., McQuiston, S., MacTurk, R.H., McCarthy, M.E., Klein, R.P., & Vietze, P.M. (1983). Assessment of mastery motivation during the first year of life: Contemporaneous and cross-age relationships. *Developmental Psychology, 19,* 159–171.

Photocopiable Forms

Activity Planning Matrix for Encouraging Engagement (APMEE)

Planning directions: When lessons have been tentatively planned, use this matrix to check (√) planning considerations addressed for each activity. For example, if you have a plan for ensuring that materials are accessible during the arrival activity, check the appropriate cell. If the planning consideration is not addressed, leave the cell blank. For each activity, complete the "Which child?" cells by putting the name or initials of a particular child for whom that planning consideration is important. See the end of the form for use of the APMEE as a post-hoc checklist.

	Activity											
Planning consideration	Arrival	Circle/ Story	Art	Snack	Outside	Centers	Free play	Toileting	Dance/ Music	Dress-up	Sand and water	Transition
Materials accessible to all?												
Which child?												
Incidental teaching?												
Which child?												
Interesting activity?												
Which child?												
Challenge?												
Which child?												
Address persistence?												
Which child?												

(continued)

McWilliam, R.A. (2005). *Activity Planning Matrix for Encouraging Engagement (APMEE).* Nashville: Vanderbilt University Medical Center, Center for Child Development.

	Activity											
Planning consideration	Arrival	Circle/ Story	Art	Snack	Outside	Centers	Free play	Toileting	Dance/ Music	Dress-up	Sand and water	Transition
Obvious goal?												
Which child?												
Observe and back off?												
Which child?												
Least prompts?												
Which child?												
Peer interaction?												
Which child?												
Associative or cooperative behavior?												
Which child?												
Reinforce interactions?												
Which child?												

Post-hoc checklist: Using a blank APMEE, review the day or week's activities and check (√) those activities in which the planning consideration was accomplished. Leave blank the cells for those activities in which the planning consideration was not accomplished. For each activity, in the "Which child?" cells, write the name or initials of one child with whom the planning consideration was implemented in that activity.

Zone Defense Schedule

Time	Person A	Person B	Person C
8:00–8:15			
8:15–8:30			
8:30–8:45			
8:45–9:00			
9:00–9:15			
9:15–9:30			
9:30–9:45			
9:45–10:00			
10:00–10:15			
10:15–10:30			
10:30–10:45			
10:45–11:00			
11:00–11:15			
11:15–11:30			
11:30–11:45			
11:45–12:00			
12:00–12:15			
12:15–12:30			
12:30–12:45			
12:45–1:00			
1:00–1:15			
1:15–1:30			
1:30–1:45			
1:45–2:00			
2:00–2:15			
2:15–2:30			
2:30–2:45			
2:45–3:00			
3:00–3:15			
3:15–3:30			
3:30–3:45			
3:45–4:00			
4:00–4:15			
4:15–4:30			
4:30–4:45			
4:45–5:00			

Zone Defense Schedule Implementation Checklist

Instructions: Complete for each transition of the day, one day per week. For the duration of the observation period, examine the extent to which zone defense scheduling is used in the classroom.

Key: + = most of the time
± = some of the time
– = little of the time
NA = not applicable/ not observed

Date						
Present routine						
Next routine						
Number of staff present (circle)	1 2 3	1 2 3	1 2 3	1 2 3	1 2 3	1 2 3
Did the teachers...						
1. Post a written (ZDS-style) schedule?						
2. Give children a transition warning?						
3. Allow children to make transitions at an individual pace?						
4. Clearly mark the zones?						
5. Ensure an adult was available at the present routine?						
6. Ensure an adult was available at the next routine?						
7. Prepare the next routine (materials ready)?						
8. Make the next routine look/sound interesting to children?						
9. Clean up the present routine?						
10. Use the set-up role for unplanned situations?						
11. Alternate the set-up role among teachers during the day?						
12. Switch roles since last week?						
13. Focus on child engagement?						
14. Make activity lengths appropriately short?						
15. Follow the schedule of activities?						

McWilliam, R.A. (2005f). *Zone Defense Schedule Implementation Checklist.* Nashville: Vanderbilt University Medical Center, Center for Child Development. In *Engagement of Every Child in the Preschool Classroom* by R.A. McWilliam & Amy M. Casey.

Family Preparation Form

Dear ____________________________:

You will soon be meeting with the rest of the team to discuss ways we can help you and your child. During the meeting, you and the other members of the team will

1. Discuss any overall questions or concerns you have
2. Talk about what your child's day is like
3. Choose outcomes to work on
4. Plan who will work on these outcomes and when

This form will help you prepare for the meeting. You may want to look over it to see the types of information that will be useful. If you think it would help to have this information written down when you come to the meeting, complete as much of the form as you have time for.

The goal of the meeting is to talk about each routine—each different part of your child's day. The staff team members will ask questions as we discuss these routines. The meeting will be very flexible—its purpose is to talk about the things that are most important to you.

Your ideas are very important. If you have any suggestions or questions about the meeting, please share them with the rest of the team.

Please bring this form with you to the planning meeting.

Family Concerns and Routines

I. What are your main concerns? Think about questions, difficulties, or needs for both your child and your family as a whole.

____

____

____

____

____

____

____

II. What are the main routines of your family's weekday?

❍ Dressing ❍ Nap

❍ Breakfast ❍ Watching TV

❍ Leaving the house ❍ Preparing meals

❍ Household chores ❍ Evening meal

❍ Yard work ❍ Bath

❍ Lunch ❍ Bedtime

❍ Hanging out ❍ Other routines: ____________________________________

____

(continued)

McWilliam, R.A. (1992a). *The family-centered intervention plan: A routines-based approach.* Tucson, AZ: Communication Skill Builders. (Available from the author)

III. What other events occur fairly regularly or during the weekend?

- ❍ Grocery shopping
- ❍ Going to the mall
- ❍ Visiting relatives or friends
- ❍ Going to the park
- ❍ Participating in religious services
- ❍ Having visitors to the house
- ❍ Going to doctor's visits
- ❍ Using public transportation
- ❍ Going to the library
- ❍ Other routines: ______________________________

____

Family Routines Information

For each routine you've checked, think about the following questions:

- What do you do during this routine?
- What does your child do during this routine?
- How does your child affect this routine?
- How satisfied are you with this routine?

Don't write answers to these questions if you don't want to. You might just use them to guide your thoughts about each routine. Use the space below each routine for any notes that will help you discuss the routine during the team meeting.

When you discuss center or school routines with the staff, you might ask

- What does my child usually do during the routine?
- How well does my child fit into the routine?
- What specific strengths or needs does my child have in this routine?

Routine:

____

____

____

Routine:

____

____

____

Routine:

____

____

____

(continued)

McWilliam, R.A. (1992). *The family-centered intervention plan: A routines-based approach.* Tucson, AZ: Communication Skill Builders. (Available from the author)

Routine:

Routine:

Routine:

Routine:

Routine:

Routine:

Routine:

Routines-Based Interview (RBI) Report Form

Directions: This form is designed to be used to report the findings from the McWilliam model of conducting a routines-based interview. A second person (e.g., someone assisting the lead interviewer) can use the form to summarize the discussion during the interview, or it can be filled out at the end of the interview. Two sections of the report form exist: 1) an "open" form that does not specify the routine being discussed or specific questions to ask about, and 2) a "structured" form, on which home routines and exact questions are specified. This structured form is a combination of the original RBI Report Form and the Scale for Assessment of Family Enjoyment within Routines (SAFER; Scott & McWilliam, 2000).

1. Complete the information below.
2. For each routine, write a short phrase defining the routine (e.g., waking up, breakfast, hanging out, circle, snack, centers).
3. Write brief descriptions about the child's engagement in the Engagement box (e.g., participates with breakfast routine, bangs spoon on the high chair or pays attention to the teacher; names songs when asked; often leaves circle before it has ended).
4. Write brief descriptions about the child's independence in the Independence box (e.g., feeds herself with a spoon; drinks from a cup but spills a lot; sings all of the songs with the group but needs prompting to speak loudly enough).
5. Write brief descriptions about the child's communication and social competence in the Social Relationships box (e.g., looks parent in the eyes when pointing to things in the kitchen, pays attention to the teacher at circle but can't stand touching other children).
6. If the interview revealed no information about one of the three domains, circle *No information* in that domain for that routine.
7. Make extra copies of page 2.
8. Draw a star for concerns and likely intervention targets.

Child's name	
Date of birth	
Who is being interviewed	
Interviewer	
Date of interview	
What are your main concerns?	

(continued)

McWilliam, R.A. (1992a). *The family-centered intervention plan: A routines-based approach.* Tucson, AZ: Communication Skill Builders. (Available from the author)

Routine:	
Engagement: No information	
Independence: No information	
Social relationships: No information	
Home: Satisfaction with routine (circle one) 1 Not at all satisfied 2 3 Satisfied 4 5 Very satisfied	Classroom: Fit of routine and child (circle one) 1 Poor goodness of fit 2 3 Average goodness of fit 4 5 Excellent goodness of fit
Domains addressed (circle all that apply) Physical Cognitive Communication Social or emotional Adaptive	

Routine:	
Engagement: No information	
Independence: No information	
Social relationships: No information	
Home: Satisfaction with routine (circle one) 1 Not at all satisfied 2 3 Satisfied 4 5 Very satisfied	Classroom: Fit of routine and child (circle one) 1 Poor goodness of fit 2 3 Average goodness of fit 4 5 Excellent goodness of fit
Domains addressed (circle all that apply) Physical Cognitive Communication Social or emotional Adaptive	

(continued)

McWilliam, R.A. (1992a). *The family-centered intervention plan: A routines-based approach.* Tucson, AZ: Communication Skill Builders. (Available from the author)

Outcomes

Before asking the family to select "things to work on," review the concerns identified by a star on the previous pages.

Outcome (short, informal version)	Priority number

(continued)

McWilliam, R.A. (1992a). *The family-centered intervention plan: A routines-based approach.* Tucson, AZ: Communication Skill Builders. (Available from the author)

RBI-SAFER Report Combo

This report combines the Routines-Based Interview Report Form (McWilliam, 2003) and the Scale for Assessment of Family Enjoyment within Routines (Scott & McWilliam, 2000).

<table>
<tr><td colspan="2">Routine: Waking up</td></tr>
<tr><td colspan="2">• Could you describe what wake-up time is like?
• Who usually wakes up first?
• Where does your child sleep?
• How does your child let you know she is awake?
• Does she want to be picked up right away? If so, is she happy when picked up?
• Or is she content by herself for a few minutes? What does she do?
• What is the rest of the family doing at this time?
• Is this a good time of day? If not, what would you like to be different?</td></tr>
<tr><td colspan="2">Notes:</td></tr>
<tr><td colspan="2">Engagement: No information</td></tr>
<tr><td colspan="2">Independence: No information</td></tr>
<tr><td colspan="2">Social relationships: No information</td></tr>
<tr><td>Home: Satisfaction with routine (circle one)
1 Not at all satisfied
2
3 Satisfied
4
5 Very satisfied</td><td>Classroom: Fit of routine and child (circle one)
1 Poor goodness of fit
2
3 Average goodness of fit
4
5 Excellent goodness of fit</td></tr>
<tr><td colspan="2">Domains addressed (circle all that apply)
Physical Cognitive Communication Social or emotional Adaptive</td></tr>
</table>

(continued)

Routine: ***Diapering/Dressing***

- What about dressing? How does that go?
- Who helps your child dress?
- Does he help with dressing? How? What can he do on his own?
- What is his mood like?
- What is communication like?
- Does your child wear diapers?
- Are there any problems with diapering?
- What does your child do while you are changing him?
- Does your child use the toilet? How independently?
- How does he let you know when he needs to use the toilet?
- How satisfied are you with this routine? Is there anything you would like to be different?

Notes:

Engagement:	No information
Independence:	No information
Social relationships:	No information

Home: Satisfaction with routine (circle one)	Classroom: Fit of routine and child (circle one)
1 Not at all satisfied	1 Poor goodness of fit
2	2
3 Satisfied	3 Average goodness of fit
4	4
5 Very satisfied	5 Excellent goodness of fit

Domains addressed (circle all that apply)

Physical Cognitive Communication Social or emotional Adaptive

(continued)

Routine: *Feeding/Meals*

- What are feedings/mealtimes like?
- Does anyone help feed your child? Who?
- How often does she eat?
- How much can she do on her own?
- How involved is she with meals?
- Where does your child usually eat?
- What are other family members doing at this time?
- How does your child let you know what she wants or whether she is finished?
- Does she like mealtimes? How do you know?
- What would make mealtimes more enjoyable for you?
- What are mealtimes like for your child when under the care of others?

Notes:

Engagement: No information

Independence: No information

Social relationships: No information

Home: Satisfaction with routine (circle one)	Classroom: Fit of routine and child (circle one)
1 Not at all satisfied	1 Poor goodness of fit
2	2
3 Satisfied	3 Average goodness of fit
4	4
5 Very satisfied	5 Excellent goodness of fit

Domains addressed (circle all that apply)

Physical Cognitive Communication Social or emotional Adaptive

(continued)

McWilliam, R.A. (2006, January). *Routines-Based Interview (RBI) Report Form.* Nashville: Vanderbilt University Medical Center, Center for Child Development.

Routine: *Getting ready to go/Traveling*	
• How do things go when you are getting ready to go somewhere with your child? • Who usually helps your child get ready? • How much can he do on his own? • How involved is he in the whole process of getting ready to go? • What is communication like at this time? • Does your child like outings? How do you know? • Is this a stressful activity? What would make this time easier for you? • What are drop-off and pick-up times like for your child? Do you or other caregivers have any concerns?	
Notes:	
Engagement: No information	
Independence: No information	
Social relationships: No information	
Home: Satisfaction with routine (circle one) 1 Not at all satisfied 2 3 Satisfied 4 5 Very satisfied	Classroom: Fit of routine and child (circle one) 1 Poor goodness of fit 2 3 Average goodness of fit 4 5 Excellent goodness of fit
Domains addressed (circle all that apply) Physical Cognitive Communication Social or emotional Adaptive	

(continued)

Routine: *Hanging out/Watching TV*

- What does your family do when relaxing at home?
- How is your child involved in this activity?
- How does your child interact with other family members?
- Does your family watch TV? Will your child watch TV?
- What does he like to watch? How long will he watch TV?
- Do you have a favorite show?
- Is there anything you would like to do in the evening but can't?

Notes:

Engagement: No information

Independence: No information

Social relationships: No information

Home: Satisfaction with routine (circle one)	Classroom: Fit of routine and child (circle one)
1 Not at all satisfied	1 Poor goodness of fit
2	2
3 Satisfied	3 Average goodness of fit
4	4
5 Very satisfied	5 Excellent goodness of fit

Domains addressed (circle all that apply)

Physical Cognitive Communication Social or emotional Adaptive

(continued)

McWilliam, R.A. (2006, January). *Routines-Based Interview (RBI) Report Form.* Nashville: Vanderbilt University Medical Center, Center for Child Development.

Routine: *Bath time*	
• What is bath time like? • Who usually helps your child bathe? • How is your child positioned in the bathtub? • Does she like the water? How do you know? • How involved is your child in bathing herself or playing in the water? • Does she kick or splash in the water? • What toys does she like to play with in the tub? • How does she communicate with you? What do you talk about? • Is bath time usually a good time? If not, what would make it better?	
Notes:	
Engagement:	No information
Independence:	No information
Social relationships:	No information
Home: Satisfaction with routine (circle one) 1 Not at all satisfied 2 3 Satisfied 4 5 Very satisfied	Classroom: Fit of routine and child (circle one) 1 Poor goodness of fit 2 3 Average goodness of fit 4 5 Excellent goodness of fit
Domains addressed (circle all that apply) Physical Cognitive Communication Social or emotional Adaptive	

(continued)

Routine: *Nap/Bedtime*

- How does bedtime go?
- Who usually puts your child to bed?
- Do you read books or have some type of ritual at this time?
- How does he fall asleep?
- How does your child calm himself?
- Does he sleep through the night? What happens if he wakes up? Who gets up with him?
- Is bedtime an easy or stressful time for your family?
- Does he take naps for other caregivers? How does that go?

Notes:

Engagement: No information

Independence: No information

Social relationships: No information

Home: Satisfaction with routine (circle one)	Classroom: Fit of routine and child (circle one)
1 Not at all satisfied	1 Poor goodness of fit
2	2
3 Satisfied	3 Average goodness of fit
4	4
5 Very satisfied	5 Excellent goodness of fit

Domains addressed (circle all that apply)

Physical Cognitive Communication Social or emotional Adaptive

(continued)

McWilliam, R.A. (2006, January). *Routines-Based Interview (RBI) Report Form.* Nashville: Vanderbilt University Medical Center, Center for Child Development.

Routine: *Grocery store*	
• How are trips to the grocery store? Do you bring your child with you? • Does she sit in a shopping cart? • Does she like being at the store? • How is she involved in shopping? Do you have to occupy her, or is she pretty content? • How does she react to other people in the store? • How does she communicate with you and others at this time? • Is there anything that would make shopping with your child easier?	
Notes:	
Engagement: No information	
Independence: No information	
Social relationships: No information	
Home: Satisfaction with routine (circle one) 1 Not at all satisfied 2 3 Satisfied 4 5 Very satisfied	Classroom: Fit of routine and child (circle one) 1 Poor goodness of fit 2 3 Average goodness of fit 4 5 Excellent goodness of fit
Domains addressed (circle all that apply) Physical Cognitive Communication Social or emotional Adaptive	

(continued)

McWilliam, R.A. (2006, January). *Routines-Based Interview (RBI) Report Form.* Nashville: Vanderbilt University Medical Center, Center for Child Development. In *Engagement of Every Child in the Preschool Classroom* by R.A. McWilliam & Amy M. Casey.

Routine: *Outdoors*	
• Does your family spend much time outdoors? What do you do? • What does your child do? • Does your child like (the activity)? • How does he get around? • How does he interact with others? • Are there any toys or games he engages with/in? • How does your child let you know when he wants to do something different? • What things does your child like or notice outside? • Is this usually an enjoyable time? Would anything help make this time easier? • What kinds of outdoor activities does he participate in? How much assistance does he need? How does he interact with his peers?	
Notes:	
Engagement: No information	
Independence: No information	
Social relationships: No information	
Home: Satisfaction with routine (circle one) 1 Not at all satisfied 2 3 Satisfied 4 5 Very satisfied	Classroom: Fit of routine and child (circle one) 1 Poor goodness of fit 2 3 Average goodness of fit 4 5 Excellent goodness of fit
Domains addressed (circle all that apply) Physical Cognitive Communication Social or emotional Adaptive	

(continued)

McWilliam, R.A. (2006, January). *Routines-Based Interview (RBI) Report Form.* Nashville: Vanderbilt University Medical Center, Center for Child Development.

Routines-Based Interview Implementation Checklist

Interviewer: ______________________ Date: ______________________

Observer: ______________________ Parent's initials: ______________________

Directions: Beside each item, check one of the five choices. At the end of the observation, add the checks in each of the five columns and enter the totals at the end of the respective columns. Better implemented interviews have higher totals for the Often and Always columns, compared with the other three columns. With repeated observations, the goal is to have as many items as possible checked in the Often and Always columns.

	Never	Sometimes	Half of the time	Often	Always
1. Did the interview have a good flow (conversational, not a lot of time spent writing)?					
2. Were both the interviewer and the parent engaged in the conversation (not distracted by other things that were going on, not looking around the room)?					
3. Did the interviewer ask follow-up questions to gain an understanding of functioning?					
4. Did the interviewer address all of the family's routines, especially by following the parent's lead?					
5. Were follow-up questions related to engagement?					
6. Were follow-up questions related to independence?					
7. Were follow-up questions related to social relationships?					
8. Were follow-up questions developmentally appropriate?					
9. Were open-ended questions used initially to gain an understanding of the routine and functioning (followed by closed questions if necessary)?					
10. Did the interviewer find out what people in the family other than the child are doing in each routine?					
11. Did the interviewer ask for a rating for each routine?					

(continued)

Rasmussen, J.L., & McWilliam, R.A. (2006). *RBI Implementation Checklist.* Nashville: Vanderbilt University Medical Center, Center for Child Development.

	Never	Sometimes	Half of the time	Often	Always
12. Did the interviewer find out, beyond the rating, how satisfied the family is with each routine?					
13. In the transition between routines, was the question *What happens next?* or something similar used?					
14. Did the interviewer use good affect (facial expressions, tone of voice, responsiveness)?					
15. Did the interviewer use affirming behaviors (nodding, positive comments, gestures)?					
16. Did the interviewer attempt to get the parent's perspective on behaviors (why the parent thinks the child does what he or she does)?					
17. Did the interviewer use active listening techniques (rephrasing, clarifying, summarizing)?					
18. If there were no problems in the routine, did the interviewer ask what the parent would like to see next?					
19. Did the interviewer avoid unnecessary questions, such as the specific time something occurs?					
20. Did the interviewer find out how the parent feels about certain behaviors?					
21. Did the interviewer act in a nonjudgmental way?					
22. Did the interviewer use "time of day" instead of "routine"?					
23. Did the interviewer return easily to the interview after an interruption?					
24. Did the interviewer allow the parent to state his or her own opinions, concerns, and so forth (not leading the family toward what the interviewer thinks is important)?					
25. Did the interviewer get information about activities outside the home (religious activities, meetings, grocery shopping)?					
26. Did the interviewer get information on the parent's down time (any time for him- or herself)?					
TOTAL					

Goal Functionality Scale II

Directions: This scale is designed to rate one individualized family service plan (IFSP) outcome or individualized education plan (IEP) objective at a time. Because IEP goals are often statements about the domain addressed (e.g., Johnny will improve in communication), they barely serve as behavioral goals. The appropriate behavioral goal, therefore, is the more specific short-term objective, sometimes known as a benchmark.

1. Complete the three top-left boxes. Assign a number to each goal/objective.
2. Circle one of the five domains in the top-right box.
3. Items 1–3: Circle the appropriate usefulness score for the outcome/objective (i.e., 5, 4, or 3).
4. Items 4–11: Circle the scores matching the content of the outcome/objective. Note that functional domains are engagement (E), independence (I), and social relationships (SR).
5. Items 12–20: Circle the scores matching the flaws in the outcome/objective.
6. Score: Beginning with the general usefulness score (5, 4, or 3), add 1 for each +1 that is circled and subtract 1 for each –1 that is circled. Enter the resulting score in the score box. This score could be a negative integer (e.g., –2).

Child's name/ID:	Domain (circle one):
Goal/objective #:	Cognitive Communication Motor Social-emotional Adaptive
Rater's initials:	

Item	Score
1. Is this goal GENERALLY USEFUL (i.e., can you answer *why* and *who cares*; broad enough yet specific enough)? If YES,	5
2. ...NOT REALLY USEFUL? If YES,	4
3. ...NOT AT ALL USEFUL? If YES,	3

Item	Score	Item	Score
4. Addresses **duration** of interaction with people or objects (E)	+1	12. Cannot tell in what normalized **contexts** it would be useful	–1
5. Persistence (E)	+1	13. Purpose is not evident or useful	–1
6. Developmentally and contextually appropriate **construction** (E)	+1	14. Some element makes little sense	–1
7. Pragmatic **communication** (SR)	+1	15. Unnecessary skill	–1
8. Naturalistic **social interaction** (SR)	+1	16. Jargon	–1
9. **Friendship** (SR)	+1	17. Increase/decrease	–1
10. Developmentally appropriate **independence** in routines (not just a reflection of prompt level) (I)	+1	18. Vague	–1
11. **Participation** in developmentally appropriate activities (E)	+1	19. Insufficient criterion	–1
SCORE		20. Criterion present but does not reflect a useful level of behavior	–1

McWilliam, R.A. (2005d). *Goal Functionality Scale II.* Nashville: Vanderbilt University Medical Center, Center for Child Development.

Incidental Teaching Checklist

Instructions: Each column of the checklist represents one observed routine; therefore, an observation of about 15 minutes should occur before each column is completed. Observe one adult's interactions with children. If the rate of interaction is too low to judge the use of incidental teaching, do not complete. Indicate + for "completed well"; ± for "completed to an extent"; and – for "not completed or completed inadequately."

Date: ______________________________ Observer: ______________________________

Routine: ______________________________ Teacher: ______________________________

Did the teacher...					
1. Ensure that the children had interesting things to do or talk about? (If the activity was boring, mark –.)					
2. Plan developmentally appropriate activities?					
3. Rotate activities and vary materials?					
4. Initiate interactions based on what the children were doing?					
5. Allow the children to remain engaged in the activity of their choice (i.e., not redirect the children to a new activity)?					
6. Elicit the children's elaboration of their engagement?					
Was the elaboration mostly...					
More engagement? (mark M)					
Higher engagement level? (mark H)					
Planned skill development? (mark S)					
7. Give the children no more than the amount of help they needed?					
8. Ensure that children were interested in something throughout the interaction or activity?					
9. Ensure that the children were reinforced (naturally or by the teacher) for improving their engagement?					

McWilliam, R.A. (2005e). *Incidental Teaching Checklist.* Nashville: Vanderbilt University Medical Center, Center for Child Development.

Checklist for Teachers—Consulting with a Specialist

Did I

____ Discuss, on the first visit, how consultation will be provided in the future (e.g., at the beginning and end of each session, by telephone, by e-mail, in weekly meetings)?

____ Review the child's individualized family service plan (IFSP) or (individualized education program (IEP) so I'm aware of the family's priorities?

____ Tell the specialist my concerns and priorities (e.g., "I'm not sure how to use this equipment," "The child is having trouble participating in outdoor play because of...")?

____ Report on any progress or difficulty the child has displayed in the classroom (e.g., "I've noticed that the child is sliding down in her seat, making it difficult for her to eat. What do you suggest?")?

____ Discuss which goals will be addressed?

____ Ask the specialist if any changes in activities should be made (e.g., "Do you think the child could try using his walker when we...")?

____ Ask the specialist for feedback (e.g., "Is there anything I should do differently?")?

____ Ask the specialist for clarification on interventions that I should be implementing (e.g., "I have not felt comfortable using...")?

____ Ask the specialist to clarify terms and techniques that I do not understand?

____ Thank the specialist for his or her time (e.g., "I appreciate the information you shared with me today")?

National Individualizing Preschool Inclusion Project. (2005). *Consultation checklist.* Nashville: Vanderbilt University Medical Center, Center for Child Development.

The Intervention Matrix

Child's name: ______________________ ID: ______________________ Begin date: ________ End date: ________

Directions:

1. List the IFSP/IEP goals in brief form in the Objective column, according to priority order.
2. Indicate the person responsible (T = teacher; F = family; SC = service coordinator; SE = special educator; SLP = speech-language pathologist; PT = physical therapist; OT = occupational therapist).
3. Place a √ in the grid squares corresponding to the routines in which to focus on each goal. Be realistic. Generally, the higher priority goals have more routines planned than do lower priority goals.
4. In the right-hand column, enter the number of routines planned for each goal.
5. Across the bottom, enter the number of goals targeted in each routine.
6. Add either the right-hand column or the bottom row to determine the total number of teaching opportunities. Enter the total in the bottom right-hand grid.
7. Give a copy to the family, hang one in the classroom to serve as a reminder, and file one with the IFSP/IEP.

Priority #	Person responsible	Objective	Arrival	Free play	Meals	Structured activity	Circle	Music	Art	Outdoors	Transitions	Nap	Personal hygiene	Home	Routines planned
1															
2															
3															
4															
5															
6															
7															
8															
Goals targeted in each routine															

McWilliam, R.A. (1992a). *Family-centered intervention planning: A routines-based approach.* Tucson, AZ: Communication Skill Builders. (available from the author)

Examination of the Implementation of Embedded Intervention, through Observation (EIEIO)

Directions: Identify and write on the form seven target goals from the child's individualized family service plan (IFSP) or individualized education program (IEP). Number the goals 1 through 7 in the leftmost column of the form. Photocopy the form in order to have a total of eight Routine columns for recording data. The columns to the right of the target goals represent 15-minute intervals of observation. At the top of each of the eight columns, identify the routine in which the child participated for the majority of the interval. The seven goals in the leftmost column of the form and eight activities in the top row of the form create a grid; each block within the grid represents a specific goal and a specific activity within the observation. Each block within the grid contains three columns labeled C, W, and A. Mark a Y (yes) or N (no) in each space.

- In the **C** space, indicate whether the goal **could** have been addressed. Did the structure of the activity make it possible for the goal to be addressed?
- In the **W** space, indicate whether the goal **was** addressed in the activity.
- In the **A** space, indicate whether the goal was addressed **appropriately** (place a mark in this space only if the goal was addressed). When determining if a goal was addressed appropriately, consider the developmental, individual, and contextual appropriateness of the goal. In other words, ask yourself the following:

  Is the child developmentally ready for the skill?

  Is he or she capable of demonstrating the skill?

  Was the least intrusive intervention strategy used?

  Was the goal addressed during a routine in which it was needed?

  Was the goal relevant to what the other children were doing?

The 2-hour observation is comprised of eight 15-minute intervals. Include a variety of routines within the observation so that data are representative of how often goals are being addressed throughout the day. Observations may be completed in eight consecutive intervals or at various times of the day.

Data can be used to 1) identify which goals should be targeted in particular routines, 2) determine the frequency with which goals are addressed, 3) determine which goals are most functional (those that are easily addressed within daily routines) and which goals need to be revised, and 4) plan for embedding instruction more effectively in future routines.

McWilliam, R.A., & Scott, S. (2001). *Examination of the Implementation of Embedded Intervention, through Observation* (EIEIO). Chapel Hill: The University of North Carolina, FPG Child Development Institute.

Examination of the Implementation of Embedded Intervention, through Observation (EIEIO)

Center: ______________________ Class: ______________________ Teacher: ______________________

Child: ______________________ Date: ______________________ Observer: ______________________

	Routine:				Routine:				Routine:				Routine:			
Goals	C	W	A	Notes	C	W	A	Notes	C	W	A	Notes	C	W	A	Notes

McWilliam, R.A., & Scott, S. (2001). *Examination of the Implementation of Embedded Intervention, through Observation* (EIEIO). Chapel Hill: The University of North Carolina, FPG Child Development Institute.
In *Engagement of Every Child in the Preschool Classroom* by R.A. McWilliam & Amy M. Casey.

Vanderbilt Ecological Congruence of Teaching Opportunities in Routines (VECTOR), Classroom Version

Rationale

Ecological congruence is a measure of the fit between the provision of particular types of supports and the need for those supports. When assessing the fit between a child and his or her environment, the *opportunities* (O) available in the environment must be considered, as well as the frequency with which the child takes *advantage* (A) of the opportunities. Opportunities may be provided in the physical environment or by the adults present in the environment. Incongruence is found when the opportunities being provided do not fit with the child's use of supports; too few opportunities are provided by adults or the physical environment, or the child is not taking advantage of the opportunities provided. Incongruence between a child and his or her environment can be resolved by making changes in the environment, changing the expectations for the child or activity, or intervening with the child to teach a particular skill. The VECTOR is designed to focus assessment of ecological congruence on three developmental domains: engagement, independence, and peer interactions.

Population and Setting

The VECTOR, Classroom Version, is designed to be used with children 18 months old to school age in a group setting. There is no prescribed schedule for when to use the VECTOR. It could be completed

- Periodically to monitor fit and determine potential changes needed in the environment and adult interventions
- To monitor child progress
- When particular concerns have been identified

Completing the Scale

- Observe the child for at least 10 minutes during each of the routines applicable to the child's group setting.
- For each of the 10 routines, rate nine items concerning the environment, adult interventions, and the child's performance.
- For environment and adult interventions, rate the frequency with which each routine provides the opportunities referred to with the scale from 1 (rarely) to 5 (most of the time). Record the numbers in the corresponding white boxes.
- Rate the child's performance, using the same scale, indicating if the child takes advantage of the opportunities provided.

Scoring

- Rate 9 items across 10 routines.
- For each routine (i.e., looking down each column), sum the scores for opportunity (O). Enter the sum in the Totals row and, after dividing by 6, enter the final score in the Scores row.
- For each routine (i.e., looking down each column), sum the scores for advantage (A). Enter the sum in the Totals row and, after dividing by 3, enter the final score in the Scores row.
- Across each row, sum the scores for opportunity (O; for environment and adults separately) across all routines. Enter the sum in the Totals column and, after dividing by 10, enter the final score in the Scores column.
- Across each row, sum the scores for advantage (A; child only) across all routines. Enter the sum in the Totals column and, after dividing by 10, enter the final score in the Scores column.
- Analyze the scores based on information provided on the next page.
- Implement changes and monitor success.

Casey, A.M., Freund, P.J., & McWilliam, R.A. (2004). *Vanderbilt Ecological Congruence of Teaching Opportunities in Routines (VECTOR)—Classroom Version.* Nashville: Vanderbilt University Medical Center, Center for Child Development.

Analyses

Determine the overall goodness of fit between the child and his or her environment.

Look at the bottom row (Totals). If the scores are consistently high (e.g., Opportunity scores are 5 or 6 and Advantage scores are 3), the fit is most likely good. If the scores are consistently low (e.g., Opportunity scores are 1 or 2 and Advantage scores are 1) or Opportunity and Advantage scores are dissimilar (e.g., one is high and one is low), the fit may not be good. Further analysis is needed (see items below).

Assess the fit between the environment and the child for specific routines.

Look at the bottom row. Compare Opportunity and Advantage scores within each routine. If the Opportunity and the Advantage scores for a routine are both low, look within the column of data to determine where environmental changes may be needed (in the physical environment, in adult interventions, or in both the physical environment and adult interventions).

Determine whether the child is taking advantage of the opportunities provided by the physical environment and by adults.

Look at the bottom row. Compare Opportunity and Advantage scores within each routine. If Advantage scores are low and Opportunity scores are notably higher, the child may not be taking full advantage of the opportunities provided. The discrepancy may be the result of skill deficits or challenging behaviors. Examine the data within the column to identify the specific area of concern (engagement, independence, or peer interactions).

Assess the child's engagement, independence, and peer interactions.

Look at the far right-hand column. Compare the child's Opportunity scores for engagement, independence, and peer interactions. If one of these domains (e.g., independence) has lower Opportunity scores than the other two (e.g., engagement and peer interactions), consider changing the physical environment and adult behavior so the child has more opportunities to be independent. Likewise, if Opportunity scores are high across the domains but the Advantage score is low in one or more domains, consider intervening with the child to teach particular skills.

Note: In some instances, you might find that Advantage scores are higher than Opportunity scores. In these cases, making specific changes to the environment might not be necessary for the child, although enriching the environment might further enhance the child's learning experiences.

Casey, A.M., Freund, P.J., & McWilliam, R.A. (2004). *Vanderbilt Ecological Congruence of Teaching Opportunities in Routines (VECTOR)—Classroom Version.* Nashville: Vanderbilt University Medical Center, Center for Child Development.

Vanderbilt Ecological Congruence of Teaching Opportunities in Routines (VECTOR), Classroom Version

Rating scale				
1	2	3	4	5
Rarely		Some of the time		Most of the time

Child: ______ Teacher: ______ Observer: ______ Observer's role: ______ Date: ______

Typical day for the child? ❍ Yes ❍ No If not typical, why? ______

		Arrival		Free play		Meals/ snacks		Circle		Structured activities		Outdoor activity		Centers		Personal hygiene		Storytime		Movement and music		Totals	Scores
		O	A	O	A	O	A	O	A	O	A	O	A	O	A	O	A	O	A	O	A		
Engagement	**Environment** 1. Physical environment and available materials promote engagement.																					/10	
	Adults 2. Adults are responsive to the child and consistently promote higher levels of engagement.																					/10	
	Child 3. Child is consistently engaged at his or her most sophisticated level.																					/10	
Independence	**Environment** 4. Routine allows independence.																					/10	
	Adults 5. Adults provide the least prompts necessary for independence.																					/10	
	Child 6. Child completes routine independently.																					/10	
Peer interaction	**Environment** 7. The routine provides multiple opportunities for peer interaction.																					/10	
	Adults 8. Adults promote and reinforce peer interactions.																					/10	
	Child 9. Child interacts frequently and appropriately with peers.																					/10	
	Totals	/6	/3	/6	/3	/6	/3	/6	/3	/6	/3	/6	/3	/6	/3	/6	/3	/6	/3	/6	/3		
	Scores																						

Casey, A.M., Freund, P.J., & McWilliam, R.A. (2004). *Vanderbilt Ecological Congruence of Teaching Opportunities in Routines (VECTOR)—Classroom Version.* Nashville: Vanderbilt University Medical Center, Center for Child Development.

Engagement Check II Data Collection

Interval	Number present	Number nonengaged	Number engaged	Percentage engaged	Notes
1					
2					
3					
4					
5					
6					
7					
8					
9					
10					
11					
12					
13					
14					
15					
16					
17					
18					
19					
20					
21					
22					
23					
24					
25					
26					
27					
28					
29					
30					

(continued)

McWilliam, R.A. (1999). *Engagement Check II*. Chapel Hill: The University of North Carolina, FPG Child Development Institute.

Interval	Number present	Number nonengaged	Number engaged	Percentage engaged	Notes
31					
32					
33					
34					
35					
36					
37					
38					
39					
40					
41					
42					
43					
44					
45					
46					
47					
48					
49					
50					
51					
52					
53					
54					
55					
56					
57					
58					
59					
60					
		Average percentage engaged			

McWilliam, R.A. (1999). *Engagement Check II.* Chapel Hill: The University of North Carolina, FPG Child Development Institute.

Scale for Teachers' Assessment of Routines Engagement (STARE)

Directions: Observe the child for 10 minutes in each of the following routines. First, circle the amount of time the child is engaged with adults, peers, and materials. Second, circle the complexity of the child's engagement. There is space to add additional or alternate routines at the end of the scale.

Arrival	Almost none of the time	Little of the time	Half of the time	Much of the time	Almost all of the time
With Adults	1	2	3	4	5
With Peers	1	2	3	4	5
With Materials	1	2	3	4	5
Complexity*	Nonengaged 1	Unsophisticated 2	Average 3	Advanced 4	Sophisticated 5

Circle time	Almost none of the time	Little of the time	Half of the time	Much of the time	Almost all of the time
With Adults	1	2	3	4	5
With Peers	1	2	3	4	5
With Materials	1	2	3	4	5
Complexity*	Nonengaged 1	Unsophisticated 2	Average 3	Advanced 4	Sophisticated 5

Centers/free play	Almost none of the time	Little of the time	Half of the time	Much of the time	Almost all of the time
With Adults	1	2	3	4	5
With Peers	1	2	3	4	5
With Materials	1	2	3	4	5
Complexity*	Nonengaged 1	Unsophisticated 2	Average 3	Advanced 4	Sophisticated 5

*Nonengaged = inappropriate behavior; Unsophisticated = repetitive play, casually looking around; Average = following routines, participating; Advanced = talking, creating; Sophisticated = symbolic talk, pretending, persisting.

(continued)

McWilliam, R.A. (2000). *Scale for Teachers' Assessment of Routines Engagement.* Chapel Hill: The University of North Carolina, FPG Child Development Institute.

Teacher-directed activity	Almost none of the time	Little of the time	Half of the time	Much of the time	Almost all of the time
With Adults	1	2	3	4	5
With Peers	1	2	3	4	5
With Materials	1	2	3	4	5
Complexity*	Nonengaged 1	Unsophisticated 2	Average 3	Advanced 4	Sophisticated 5

Snack/Lunch	Almost none of the time	Little of the time	Half of the time	Much of the time	Almost all of the time
With Adults	1	2	3	4	5
With Peers	1	2	3	4	5
With Materials	1	2	3	4	5
Complexity*	Nonengaged 1	Unsophisticated 2	Average 3	Advanced 4	Sophisticated 5

Outside play	Almost none of the time	Little of the time	Half of the time	Much of the time	Almost all of the time
With Adults	1	2	3	4	5
With Peers	1	2	3	4	5
With Materials	1	2	3	4	5
Complexity*	Nonengaged 1	Unsophisticated 2	Average 3	Advanced 4	Sophisticated 5

*Nonengaged = inappropriate behavior; Unsophisticated = repetitive play, casually looking around; Average = following routines, participating; Advanced = talking, creating; Sophisticated = symbolic talk, pretending, persisting.

(continued)

Routine:	Almost none of the time	Little of the time	Half of the time	Much of the time	Almost all of the time
With Adults	1	2	3	4	5
With Peers	1	2	3	4	5
With Materials	1	2	3	4	5
Complexity*	Nonengaged 1	Unsophisticated 2	Average 3	Advanced 4	Sophisticated 5

Routine:	Almost none of the time	Little of the time	Half of the time	Much of the time	Almost all of the time
With Adults	1	2	3	4	5
With Peers	1	2	3	4	5
With Materials	1	2	3	4	5
Complexity*	Nonengaged 1	Unsophisticated 2	Average 3	Advanced 4	Sophisticated 5

Routine:	Almost none of the time	Little of the time	Half of the time	Much of the time	Almost all of the time
With Adults	1	2	3	4	5
With Peers	1	2	3	4	5
With Materials	1	2	3	4	5
Complexity*	Nonengaged 1	Unsophisticated 2	Average 3	Advanced 4	Sophisticated 5

*Nonengaged = inappropriate behavior; Unsophisticated = repetitive play, casually looking around; Average = following routines, participating; Advanced = talking, creating; Sophisticated = symbolic talk, pretending, persisting.

Children's Engagement Questionnaire (CEQ)

Child's name: ______________________ Age: _____ years _____ months

Check one: ❍ Boy ❍ Girl

Rater's name: ______________________ Today's date: ______________________

Relationship to child: ❍ Mother ❍ Father ❍ Other: ______________________

Rate how this child usually spends his or her time; *typical* here should mean that the child spends quite a lot of time in this activity. The examples are only given to help understand the meaning of the items. Even though the example might not always be relevant for this child, please answer all of the questions, even if you are not sure. CIRCLE the number that best indicates how typical each statement is of this child.

	Not at all	Somewhat typical	Typical	Very typical
1. **Watches or listens to adults** *Example:* When the mother moves about the kitchen, talking to the child, the child watches her.	1	2	3	4
2. **Plays with adults who try to play with him or her** *Example:* When a family friend, someone the child knows well, begins to play with the child, the child joins in.	1	2	3	4
3. **Tries to get adults to do things** *Example:* The child tries to get the teacher to give him or her a toy.	1	2	3	4
4. **Tries to get other children to do things** *Example:* The child keeps asking another child to play on the swings.	1	2	3	4
5. **Plays with toys** *Example:* When the child is near toys, he or she plays with them.	1	2	3	4
6. **Tries to complete things, even if it takes a long time to finish** *Example:* The child knows how to put together simple jigsaw puzzles and puts together the puzzle until it is completed.	1	2	3	4
7. **Plays with objects in a simple manner (i.e., repetitive, unchanging)** *Example:* The child bangs the toy car over and over again on the highchair tray.	1	2	3	4

(continued)

	Not at all	Somewhat typical	Typical	Very typical
8. **Talks about things that happened in the past or in the future** *Example:* The child refers to an event that happened the day before. This only refers to events 24 hours or more in the past or in the future.	1	2	3	4
9. **Tries out new ways of playing with objects** *Example:* The child already knows how to roll a ball; now he or she tries to sit on it.	1	2	3	4
10. **Plays appropriately for his or her developmental level** *Example:* The child who does most things at the 2-year-old level plays with objects and people at the 2-year-old level.	1	2	3	4
11. **Tries to get toys to work** *Example:* The child works at turning the jack-in-the-box handle to get the clown to pop out.	1	2	3	4
12. **Watches or listens to other children** *Example:* When other children are playing, the child follows their movements with his or her eye gaze.	1	2	3	4
13. **Plays with other children** *Example:* When other children are nearby, the child joins in what they are doing.	1	2	3	4
14. **Stays busy** *Example:* When no adult is playing with the child, he or she finds something to do.	1	2	3	4
15. **Uses repetitive vocalizations** *Example:* The child says, "Ba-ba-ba-ba-ba."	1	2	3	4
16. **Tries out new ways of communicating or uses new language** *Example:* The child practices using new words he or she has heard from the parents.	1	2	3	4
17. **Seems constantly aware of what is going on around him or her** *Example:* The child looks at the source of noises and at moving objects and people.	1	2	3	4
18. **Solves problems quickly** *Example:* When a toy falls behind the furniture, the child rapidly finds a way to retrieve it.	1	2	3	4

(continued)

	Not at all	Somewhat typical	Typical	Very typical
19. **Plays with adults** *Example:* When adults are nearby, the child talks to them or approaches them.	1	2	3	4
20. **Figures out how things work, without asking for help** *Example:* When the child opens a present, he or she tries to play with the unfamiliar toy without adult help.	1	2	3	4
21. **Uses understandable language or sign language** *Example:* The child uses words someone other than the parents understands.	1	2	3	4
22. **Pretends to be things or other people.** *Example:* The child creeps on the floor and says, "Meow."	1	2	3	4
23. **Plays with objects the way they were intended to be played with** *Example:* The child bangs blocks with a toy hammer rather than chewing them.	1	2	3	4
24. **Continues repetitive movements to make sounds with an object** *Example:* When the child discovers that the toy rattles, he or she makes it rattle again.	1	2	3	4
25. **Concentrates hard a lot of the time** *Example:* When coloring, the child leans over the paper, keeps his or her eyes on the task, and appears to be thinking about the coloring.	1	2	3	4
26. **Chooses difficult things to do** *Example:* The child goes to the toys that require a little effort.	1	2	3	4
27. **Plays with other children who try to play with him or her** *Example:* When another child approaches, the child will talk to or play with him or her.	1	2	3	4
28. **Does what is expected (for this child), considering the time of day, place, or activity** *Example:* The child puts on clothes in the morning, goes to the bathroom in the bathroom, and plays on the seesaw during outside play.	1	2	3	4

(continued)

McWilliam, R.A. (1991). *Children's Engagement Questionnaire (CEQ)*. Chapel Hill: The University of North Carolina, FPG Child Development Institute.

	Not at all	Somewhat typical	Typical	Very typical
29. **Notices changes in people, objects, and the environment as a whole** *Example:* The child communicates, "Where's the TV?" when it is moved.	1	2	3	4
30. **Pretends objects are something else** *Example:* The child pretends a box is a car or uses an oblong block as a baby bottle.	1	2	3	4
31. **Explores objects or places** *Example:* The child turns objects over, looking inside.	1	2	3	4
32. **Tries to get adults to repeat things** *Example:* When the adult has done something the child likes, the child begs for more.	1	2	3	4

Scoring

Competent engagement: Calculate the mean of the unshaded items (4, 6, 8, 9, 10, 11, 13, 14, 16, 18, 19, 20, 21, 22, 23, 25, 26, 27, 28, 29, 30, 31, 32).

Unsophisticated engagement: Calculate the mean of the shaded items (1, 2, 3, 5, 7, 12, 15, 17, 24).

Interpretation: Unsophisticated engagement might be expected of younger children—those who do not spend as much time engaged in purposeful play with adults, peers, and materials. Intervention should be aimed at increasing the mean rating for competent engagement.

Index

Page numbers followed by *f* indicate figures; those followed by *t* indicate tables.